A COURTSHIP HANDBOOK FOR CHRISTIAN LADIES

Dovetta Marie Price
ROBINSON

© Copyright 2009-2012 Dovetta Marie Price Robinson

All rights reserved.

No part of this book may be reproduced or transmitted in any form or by any means, electronic or mechanical, including photocopy, recording, or any information storage or retrieval system, except for brief passages in connection with a critical review, without permission in writing from the author.

Library of Congress Control Number: 2008911898
ISBN: 978-0-615-30798-5

Cover and Book Design by Dr. William L. Pettiford III
Manufactured in the United States of America

Please address all requests for copies, information or permission to use to:
E-mail: **DovettaRobinson@bellsouth.net**

This book is dedicated to the ONE and ONLY true and living God, in the person of our Lord and Savior Jesus Christ [יהושע המשיח Yahushua HaMoshiach].

We give all glory, honor and praise to the Spirit of Christ who has graced us with the tongue of the ready writer. Blessed be Yahuah [יהוה] my strength, who teaches my hands to war and my fingers to fight. Thank you, Heavenly Father for the confidence to believe I can do all things through Christ who strengthens me.

I waited patiently for Yahuah [יהוה]; and he inclined unto me, and heard my cry. He brought me up also out of an horrible pit, out of the miry clay, and set my feet upon a rock, and established my goings. And he hath put a new song in my mouth, even praise unto our God [אלהים Elohim]: many shall see it, and fear, and shall trust in Yahuah [יהוה]. Blessed is that man that makes Yahuah [יהוה] his trust... Psalm 40:1-4A

To God be the Glory!

Acknowledgement

Much love to my pulchritudinous husband, K.T. for pruning my potential with your candid and silentious ways, and for watering my desires with your love and laughter. And, of course, thank you for being my sunshine on a cloudy day! – *Your Rainbow*

To the memory of my mom, my angel in disguise, Dovetta Marie Price II, truly a First Lady, one in a million dearly loved and missed. I bless God for her listening ear, enduring patience, lingering words of encouragement and her forbearing love. Her loving and God-fearing guidance has forever captivated my heart. Mom did know best! Thank you for helping me to understand that God don't pacify, he truly satisfies!

To my Dad, Bishop Dr. Reese Price Jr., with great pleasure, we are forever indebted to love and honor you and [*Mom's memory*] for introducing me to Jesus Christ.

"You told me I could do it," and I believed I could. And so I did! Much love to you and Lady Ruth Price - #7

Love to all my nine children and three grandchildren. You are the apples of mine eyes, the joys of my summer, and the security of my winter. It is my desire and prayer that you follow my example that lead to Christ. May heaven smile upon you always!

Love to all my stepchildren and step grandchildren for being so wonderful to me. We pray our special bond will never be broken. Love you much!

Love to my brothers and sisters for their love, support, laughter, inspiration, prayers, conversations, and advice. My life has been *sooooo blessed* and enriched because of you!

Thanks to my auntie mom's, Lady Vivian Purnell, Lady Gwendolyn

Wooten, and Yvonne Stevenson, for your love, counsel and guidance.

Special Acknowledgements to our sisters Miss Malia and Miss Sasha Obama, daughters of the first African American President, Mr. Barak Obama, the forty-forth President of The United States of America.

Much thanks to all who have knowingly and unknowingly contributed to the completion and success of this work!

Contents

Acknowledgements, *v*

Introduction, *ix*

RULE 1: You Are One In A Million, 11

RULE 2: Wedding Planning, 19

RULE 3: Just Smile And Keep Your Testimony, 27

RULE 4: Beware Of The Baby Doll Syndrome, 31

RULE 5: Choose God's Plan, 33

RULE 6: Read The Handwriting On The Wall, 39

RULE 7: Risk Love, 51

RULE 8: You Are Worth The Wait, 65

RULE 9: Be A Virtuous Woman, 69

RULE 10: Mood Music 101, 79

RULE 11: Courtship With Children, 87

RULE 12: Don't Be No Fool, 101

RULE 13: You Can Be A Cinderella, 109

RULE 14: Give God A Raise With Your Praise In Prayer, 115

RULE 15: Special Notes For Second Time Married Or Non-Virgins, 117

RULE 16: Pass The Salt, Please, 123

Introduction

It is my great pleasure to present *Cloud Rules* to every lovesick Christian sister who is engaged to be married. I want to congratulate your season of love. I have been there and done that, having traveled the beautiful, unforgettable, awesome, and precious road of Christian courtship. The purpose of this book is simply to help a sister out when your head is in the clouds. You are in love and love will disarm a strong man: It can make a king give up his kingdom, and a virgin [*without a promise or a ring*] give up her virginity. But I was inspired to pen for you, my lovesick sister, *Cloud Rules* because I am endeavoring to raise the bar of spiritual, social and moral excellence in Christian courtship, creating an standard for dignified Christian ladies while her head, heart, soul, spirit, and her common sense are in the clouds of love. This book is for you whether this is your first time in love or you're ready to risk loving and being loved again. *Cloud Rules* will offer many practical and spiritual nuggets to help aid and guide you in common areas of Christian courtship.

You must remember that when you are courting, you are not courting a title, position, or status, but a person of the opposite sex, a real living, breathtaking man. If you don't have your cloud rules available to warn you of the pitfalls and dangerous paths of courting, the devil has the power to ruin your godly reputation overnight. He does this because there are four things the devil wants to steal from you: your faith, your focus, your footing and your future.

Frankly, my Christian sister, it's all about keeping and maintaining your godly reputation. There is no other option. With your *Cloud Rules*, you can and you will make it to the altar even with your head in the clouds. You can have a safe landing on your feet at the altar with your God and your godly man.

RULE 1:

You Are One In A Million

"Whoso findeth a wife findeth a good thing, and obtaineth favour of Yahuah [יהוה]." Proverb 18:22

My sister this is your time and your glorious season to be blessed. Love is in the air. And just like Solomon and his love, all you see is the person you're in love with. You don't see anything or anyone else. You have found your true love, your soul mate and have great anticipation of soon becoming one joined together in the flesh. You are reflecting the beautiful story of King Solomon and the Shulamite maiden! Just as the preacher, King Solomon wooed the Shulamite maiden in the Song of Solomon, your beautiful Prince Charming is wooing you.

> [1] How beautiful you are, my darling!
> Oh, how beautiful!
> Your eyes behind your veil are doves.
> Your hair is like a flock of goats
> descending from the hills of Gilead.
> [2] Your teeth are like a flock of sheep just shorn,
> coming up from the washing.
> Each has its twin;
> not one of them is alone.
> [3] Your lips are like a scarlet ribbon;
> your mouth is lovely.
> Your temples behind your veil

> are like the halves of a pomegranate.
> ⁴ Your neck is like the tower of David,
> built with courses of stone;
> on it hang a thousand shields,
> all of them shields of warriors.
> ⁵ Your breasts are like two fawns,
> like twin fawns of a gazelle
> that browse among the lilies.
> ⁶ Until the day breaks
> and the shadows flee,
> I will go to the mountain of myrrh
> and to the hill of incense.
> ⁷ You are altogether beautiful, my darling;
> there is no flaw in you.
>
>   Songs of Solomon 4:1-7

The King is *sooooooo* in love with her. This Shulamite maiden has turned this man's head 180 degrees. He sees nothing but her beauty, no matter how much she fusses about her issue. It is comforting to know in this story of King Solomon and the Shulamite maiden the tender thoughts for his bride in her unperfected state! When your soon-to-be husband laid his eyes on you, he loved everything about you. He loved you with your freckles, moles, and pimples. Yes, he even loved your knock-knees, big eyes, big momma's feet, missing front teeth, big hips and all. Love covers a multitude of faults. You are perfect in his eyes, just as you are.

Proverb 18:22 says, "Whoso findeth a wife findeth a good thing, and obtaineth favour of Yahuah [יהוה]." The idiom in the *Merriam-Webster's Collegiate Thesaurus* defines the word find as one in a million. You are One in A Million, in the divine will and purpose of God to experience such love as the Shulamite maiden.

During your courtship and marriage preparations, remember you are his one in a million so don't be so hard on yourself that you can't enjoy the experience. Remember, Christ loved us first; who are we not to love ourselves? And just as the Shulamite maiden complained about her color, there are things you will want to change, and there will be some things you really shouldn't worry about like wishing you hadn't had your tubes tied, or neglected to have that foot surgery when you had great health insurance. Start from ground zero, and do what you can with what you have. Don't let your past dictate your future.

Remember, just as Christ loves the church so is the husband to love his wife, even as his own body. So don't stress over your outer so-called imperfections because God beautifies the meek with salvation [Psalm 149:4]. Let the inner beauty of the Holy Spirit shine through you. Your presence and womanly personage is a hand written speech of a mighty God. You are an exquisite hand made portrait, a walking thesaurus of everything gracious and divine. You are blessed, highly favored, one in a million, and altogether lovely.

> "Yes! Many are the plans in a man's heart,
> but it is the purpose of Yahuah [יהוה] that prevails."
> Proverb 19:21

So you said emphatically, "Yes! I'll marry you!" Are you ready? Are you sure? Then go buy yourself a great pair of walking shoes, cause have we got suggestions for you. Let's go girl!

Let me tell you, whatever phone plan you have, you're going to need to increase your minutes, because between talking morning, noon, and night to your love, out of town family members, and vendors for your wedding you just gotta have more minutes.

Roll up your sleeves and get busy having the most fantastic, hilariously wonderful, sincerest Christian courtship while planning the most romantic, exciting, and demanding day of your life. Okay, not so fast. First, take a deep breath, stop, think and let's put things in the proper order. You've told everybody and their momma. You're in love and your head is in the clouds. All of your natural senses are at full attention—all five of them: seeing, hearing, smelling, taste, and touch is at your front door ringing every joy bell in your heart.

Wherever you were when the proposal took place will forever be ingrained upon your heart. You will never forget the place or the day. Even the time of day will long be remembered from that time on, whether it was a morning pancake house breakfast proposal, an evening elegant candle light dinner proposal or maybe at a backyard family barbecue. You'll be saying, "I never shall forget that day. Even the darkest clouds can't keep the sunshine away." Every little girl's fairy tale dream has become your reality. Finally, your pulchritudinous prince has come for you.

Every phone conversation will be different. When you see each other even for casual lunch or a walk in the park, it will be different because you are walking with your soon-to-be husband. Don't walk, talk or move too fast. Take your good-and-plenty time because your sweet courtship will go by so fast your memory won't be able to keep accurate records. Let me remind you of the times in which we are living; wedding bells and court gavels are ringing simultaneously. One minute couples are getting married, and the next minute couples are getting divorced.

So you're getting married and that's fantastic, fabulous, wonderful, and marvelous. Now let's get you to the altar sparkling, spotless and blameless while you are high and lifted up into the clouds of love. You my sister, must carefully pace your steps and begin your courtship with blissful anticipation and serious caution so you will not end up with grave consequences of a broken heart or even spiritual suicide. Heaven has your back and I got you covered with *Cloud Rules* to assist you prayerfully to the altar [*or courthouse*] with your God and your godly man. You must stay conscious and sober, use godly wisdom, and never allow your five senses to dictate, control or manipulate your actions, thoughts or decisions in any way that would bring dishonor to you and disgrace to the Spirit of Christ. Why? Because man is triune [*three-fold*], spirit, soul, and body. Your body is the house, temple, or building in which the invisible spirit and soul live. The spirit is the real inner man, the part that knows God. The soul is the mind, or intellect, the will and emotions that is operated by the five senses of seeing, hearing, touching, tasting and smelling.

Your Christian courtship should be godly, and extremely precious. It is the closest personal relationship one can experience, to know and understand how God must feel about his bride the church. Your fiancé will ponder, "Is she trustworthy, faithful, loyal, and honest? Does she love me as much as I love her? Will she wait patiently for me until we consummate our love?"

In fact, as a Christian woman, your fiancé won't have to worry about you even when he's weak because, your loyalty will be first to God. If you are loyal and faithful to God, you will be loyal and faithful to him because of the God that is within you. This is also the kind of husband you want. If he can't hold out before you get married, then what's to keep him when you get married and you become sick or disabled and can't perform your sexual obligations or vice versa?

Let me tell you my sister, being in a Christian courtship is work naturally and spiritually. Never forget the Blesser who blessed you to have this wonderful godly experience. Enjoy, enjoy, enjoy the journey, as well as the destination. Don't let the devil steal your joy, or your shining moment before man and God. You will stand before a host of witnesses, the picture of elegance, the pride and joy of the Christian community another sister who kept it good and godly. Your fiancé will be able to say without reservation that his heart does safely trust in you.

Cloud Rules

"For I know the thoughts that I think towards you, saith Yahuah [יהוה], thoughts of peace, and not of evil, to give you an expected end."
Jeremiah 29:11

It was the last day of our sensational honeymoon. Early that morning my new husband and I had already packed and checked out of our week long stay at the Royal Sea Cliff Resort in Kona, Hawaii, so we could take advantage of the entire day. We were looking forward to our last sightseeing tour before we left the island, which happened to be a four-hour trip to the only live volcano on the island.

Hours later, after filling our hearts with the whole exuberant experience of the amazingly beautiful scenic waterfalls of the island, playing with the volcano ash, enjoying every minute of our stop-and-go-broke irresistible souvenirs purchases, taking numerous camera shots and video clips of the island, we had to now hurry back for our appointed flight back to reality, home, kids, dishes. Just before leaving The Volcano Park, our heavenly father allowed me to experience a miraculous childhood fantasy: As we were enjoying the magnificent view of the island, in an unexpected moment, God answered my childhood desires. I was able to experience firsthand, how truly wonderful and delightful clouds felt.

High on the mountaintop, we thought we were running into a soft rain. However, we began to notice that nothing was falling on the windshield as we know rain does. The precipitation was amazingly different. It looked like raindrops mixed with mist. The water on the windshield was as if we were intruding into a wet mass parked in mid-air. Then something magnificent happened: we looked down and around and realized that we were in the clouds.

As a little girl, clouds looked like balls of cotton to me; I often wondered if they felt like cotton. My little inquiring mind sincerely wanted to know. I just couldn't fathom how it could be possible to touch them. But I always believed that God could do it; and this was my heavenly set up. Oh! My childish heart was filled with joy and excitement. We traveled so high up that we drove right into the clouds. The view was like looking out the window aboard an airplane; the houses and buildings look like toys, and the black sand beaches were littered with cruise liners that looked like rowboats. I thought, "Just because I had the audacity to believe in possibilities, my childish faith literally became my reality." I put my hand out of the window while the car was still moving, and began to experience the wonder of having my hand and head literally in the clouds. How can I ever find the words to express the joy I felt not only being in the clouds, but being in the clouds with my love? All in one happy day, it came to pass. Faith, the substance of things hoped for, was now my reality.

The atmosphere in the clouds filled my heart with so much love, joy, peace and happiness that I forgot for a moment just where we were until I noticed something that made fear grip my heart. I looked just a few feet ahead of us on the two way lane on which we were traveling and notice that for stretches of road at a time, there was no parking room to my left or to my right for an idle or disabled vehicle. If we were to have a flat tire or run out of gas, we had no room to pull over for service. Both sides of the road had a suicide drop to God knows where, and I certainly didn't want to find out. As happy and exhilarating the experience was on the mountain top in the clouds, in a heartbeat, just the thought of the dangers and possible mishaps caused me to pray the LORD would bless us to get down from here as safely as we came up.

There are safety rules for being in the clouds and they don't change because you are in awe. The law of gravity says what goes up, must come down. Apostle Peter had a similar mountaintop experience with Jesus in Matthew 17:1-8

[1] After six days Jesus took with him Peter, James and John the

brother of James, and led them up a high mountain by themselves. ² There he was transfigured before them. His face shone like the sun, and his clothes became as white as the light. ³ Just then there appeared before them Moses and Elijah, talking with Jesus. ⁴ Peter said to Jesus, "Lord, it is good for us to be here. If you wish, I will put up three tabernacles—one for you, one for Moses and one for Elijah." ⁵ While he was still speaking, a bright cloud covered them, and a voice from the cloud said, "This is my Son, whom I love; with him I am well pleased. Listen to him!" ⁶ When the disciples heard this, they fell face down to the ground, terrified. ⁷ But Jesus came and touched them. "Get up," he said. "Don't be afraid." ⁸ When they looked up, they saw no one except Jesus.

Peter had to come down out of the clouds, and so did I. The best part we had in common; we were up there with Jesus. He kept us safe even in a fearful place. His promises are sure. He promised to never leave us, and that he would be with us always. We could count on Jesus to keep all his promises.

When looking down from the top of the mountain, everything was beautiful because I was looking afar off into the distance and not up close at the immediate danger. But then looking immediately in front of me showed me just how dangerous my situation was. I would like to use this analogy of being in clouds to compare with courting. As long as your head is in the clouds, everything looks beautiful afar off. But then you take a closer look at things like the frightening words of your wedding vows that you will repeat, and you realize that to vow to be with someone "For better or for worse…for richer or poorer…" means that there can certainly be a "poorer" and a "worse!"

You are in a Christian courtship, and the realities of clouds will cause you to see and hear some fearful things, especially if you are being elevated into ministry. The mountaintop experience is not a place to pick flowers. Having your head in the clouds is a place of reverence, awe, joy, and revelations. Yes, I did face fear while I was on the mountaintop, but because of my faith in God, my fear was fleeting. For God has not given us the spirit of fear, but of power and of love and of a sound mind. Being in a Christian courtship is fabulous and fearful.

I want to acknowledge and honor your glorious and admirable place. Yes, you are blessed and highly favored, and there are many sisters who desire to be in your shoes. You were singled out to be shined upon. God set his candle upon a hill, for his light to shine to the world. We Christian sisters are the light of the world. God set you up high to look at him. The world will be amazed at your honor and dignity while saying, "Look at Jesus."

RULE 2:

Wedding Planning

With that being said it's time for you to carefully select your supporting cast. Your family and friends will be your supporting cast, of helping hands, and sympathetic ears. They will help keep your wedding planning joyous and filled with laughter while having the time of your life. Most importantly, pray with your fiancé and ask God to only allow those individuals who will bring honor and glory to him on your day of love to be in the wedding.

If you have a host of individuals who will want to be in your wedding this prayer will come in handy when you don't know how to say "No," or "I'm sorry we have all the help and assistance we can handle." If you are an individual who have a hard time saying no to people, we strongly suggest that you put someone in charge that can. This individual would be your wedding coordinator, someone who will follow your directives and wishes, and has no problem in speaking on your behalf. When you are approached by individuals who want to be in your wedding, you can just tell them, "Please see my wedding coordinator."

I'm going to list many things that may become very important to you during your courtship. But, let me whisper this into your ear: I know you are so very, very, very happy and ecstatic about planning your wedding and the honeymoon, etc., but there are those [*haterators/friendlimies – defined as enemies disguised as friends*] who you may have thought were your friends and you were certain that they would be happy for you. Here's some mail from someone who has experienced this. Everyone will not be happy for you. Remember Julius Caesar, dyeing his garments in the blood of one million

of his foes, conquered 800 cities, only to be stabbed by his best friend at the scene of his greatest triumph. A teacher asked a student to sum up Socrates life in four lines. Here's what he said:
- Socrates lived long ago
- He was very intelligent
- Socrates gave long speeches and
- His friends poisoned him.

What about Jesus, our perfect example? Watch the kissers and huggers when your engagement announcement is made public. Everybody has a Judas somewhere hanging around in their circle of friends and acquaintances. Remember Psalm 23, God will prepare a table before you in the presence of your enemies. They will see but will not be able to enjoy because it's a God thing. In fact, these cloud rules are just in time. The mail has been opened and you will be able to see them coming because you read their mail. When you read later about The Spiritual Cinderella you're understand a little better.

I remember as my courtship progressed, haterators began to flock to the occasion; it was getting pretty ugly. Yup! But no sweat. Remember I was born in a fishbowl so because I was seasoned just right and one in a million, God just gave me the grace I needed to stand in the midst of it all. If as a Christian sister, you experience folks telling things that are not true about you, just bless God and remember Jesus was lied on. You have nothing to worry about, as long as it's not true. I was on display and you are on display. God was telling the devil to throw his best shot because He know I had been prepared and so are you.

A Traditional Wedding Check List

The steps of a good man are ordered by Yahuah [יהוה]:
and he delighteth in his way. Psalm 37:23

Let's assume everyone has been informed of your plans to marry. If not start sending out your informal save the date announcements. Now let's get busy with the rules! I hope I don't forget too much. This list does not have an order.

In our efforts to help you plan we suggest that you:
- Delegate
- Give deadlines
- Follow-up
- Stick to a budget
- Network

Set goals and a timeline in which you want specific tasks to be complete.

You will definitely need a writing pad, at least a five subject notebook. Keep everything related to the "To Do List" in the same place. This is vital for memory sake, a journal for your journey. Enjoy, enjoy, enjoy every moment, because nothing lasts forever. You're going to have to come down out of the clouds, sober up, and get on with the business of marriage.

Celebrate every moment, for memory sake. Take pictures of everything that makes you happy; have yourself a ball. If I could do it all over again, I would take my own advice, something I didn't think about until later. It would have certainly made my life a whole lot less complicated and tremendously more rewarding.

Things to consider when preparing for your wedding:

1. Buy a camera, or keep on hand a few instant cameras for precious courtship moments. You'll be glad you did!
2. Decide how much planning time before the big day. Six, twelve, eighteen or twenty-four months?
3. If you are on a fixed income, try and be more creative in your courtship instead of eating up your assets with a lot of dinning. Slow down the daily drive thru fast food restaurant, and eat out at a finer dining once or twice a month. In other words, if you must eat out, make it worth the wait; you will save more if you eat less often. Quality dining instead of quantity dining. This is especially helpful for weight consciousness.
4. Use a cash purchase system. Leave your credit/debit card at home, and don't leave home with it.
5. Decide how much money you can afford to spend a day and only

carry that amount no extra, if you already live on a monthly budget.
6. Don't forget to include your kids in the planning.
7. Don't be selfish; it takes two to get married. Share every planning moment with your fiancé. Remember in your courtship you are also bonding. You may be crazy about strawberry cake and he may be allergic to strawberries. As you share and prepare to live together this is a perfect opportunity to learn about likes and dislikes. In fact, the ability to listen and compromise, while respecting each other's desires will be the same skills you will need in your marriage. If they are not interested then do what you need to do, just check every now and then.
8. If your budget allows, you may want to purchase a book on planning a wedding, wedding magazines, books from your local library or internet sources. However if not, there are plenty of tips here to put you on the right path.
9. Engagement party or dinner, not necessary but traditional.
10. If you only knew your fiancé under six months and he was previously married, you may want to see proof of his divorce decree. Optional. Some pastors require proof of divorce or special permissions when remarrying. Beware, you may be asked for it during premarital counseling, which is also highly recommended, especially if marrying with children.
11. Newspaper Announcements of your wedding plans, or build your own website.
12. Brides Bouquet
13. Accommodations for out-of-town guests.
14. Wedding ring and gift for the groom.
15. Finding and selecting the perfect engagement ring. Yellow gold? Silver?
16. Buy insurance if the ring is very expensive.
17. Remember the 4 Ws:
    - **Who** and how many, will you invite, – The Guest List?
    - **What** will be your wedding style? Traditional, Romantic, Sophisticated etc?
    - **Where**, Location/site? Budget, how much will it cost?
    - **When**, Day of the week, Friday, Saturday, or Sunday? You'll need

lead time for booking. Some places are booked solid for months. Try to avoid tourist season and rush hour traffic times, etc. [*also same advice for honeymoon plans*].

18. How much is too much? What is a reasonable cost? Buy in seasons or advance purchases, and expect to compromise.
19. Have you set the date? Month, day and year?
20. Do you need a Bridal Consultant? If so get everything in writing.
21. Use a trusted referral if possible; use your instinct and common sense.
22. The wedding time? Morning, Noon, Evening?
23. Place? Destination for your wedding if your budget allows. Contact your travel agent to get ideas, or a location that already has a special meaning for you. Traditionally House of worship or Hotel, Indoor, or Outdoor. Have a plan B for outdoors.
24. Wedding Theme: for example mine was rainbow, from my program to the bridal party attire, continued throughout the reception of flower petals on the wedding cake.
25. Have you decided the season you will marry: Winter, Spring, Summer, Autumn?
26. Holiday themes: Watch out, certain holiday's can be competitive to vacations.
27. Who's going to officiate? Don't assume; talk over choices with fiancé.
28. Officiant [*preacher*] fee.
29. Your pastor or his pastor?
30. Church or site fee.
31. Flower girl basket. Keep in mind, before or after Easter, and after Prom Season is a great time to buy gloves, flowers baskets, dresses, shoes, etc.
32. Thank you notes, Reception/Response cards
33. Tuxedo rentals and who will be designated to return the grooms tux?
34. Purchase the ring pillows, toasting goblets, etc.
35. Boutonnieres for attendants and fathers.
36. Mothers' corsages
37. Reception rentals
38. Send out your Save-the-Date announcements to your entire guest list three to six months before actual wedding date.

39. Get on the phone and get those addresses corrected for mailing labels.
40. Who will do your labels for you?
41. If sending out Save-the-Date announcements, and wedding invitations will be too costly, save your stamps for the invitations?
42. Who will do the invitation? Will they be custom? Store bought!
43. Plan how you will properly write your invitation.
44. Tip: you can purchase beautiful designer paper and put your invitation on it.
45. Decorations: who will be your decorator? How much will it cost?
46. What is your budget? Will you pay for the expenses or parents, or fiancé?
47. Pictures? A professional is recommended, friends and family may be an option.
48. Open up a checking account with your name and his name on the account. People will write checks to you and to him. You can put all the checks in the same account, until you can change the account with your married name.
49. Start buying your stamps, and putting them aside.
50. Don't spend unnecessary money joining a health club. You wouldn't want to break or sprain anything before you get to the altar. Remember, when he proposed to you he loved what he saw so just cut back and enjoy the courtship. If you want to spend some money to fix something, put it on your smile.
51. Get your teeth cleaned or fixed if you can. You don't want to put your hand up to your mouth every time you see a camera, or set a freeze smile to keep from showing your teeth. Now! If you are okay with your grill, then don't let these cloud rules interfere. Smile and be happy that's the bottom line.
52. Don't forget your marriage license, take your camera, it's a Kodak moment!
53. What are you wearing? Traditional wedding dress or other? You can borrow, buy, or rent your dress. You can wear white, even if you are not a virgin! However, the veil is the symbol of virginity should not be worn, so the etiquette book says. Folks do what they want. It's your day! Have a great one!
54. Rehearsal Time – *At least three practice sessions*

55. What about your Veil? Shoes? Accessories?
56. Colors, Colors, Colors, have you picked out your bridal colors yet?
57. Wedding program, a lot of money could be saved if you buy wedding paper at an office store, you will have a beautiful selection to choose from.
58. Who will be your Maid of Honor? Matron? [*Maid is single – Matron is married*].
59. Flower girls, ring bearer.
60. Who will be the best man
61. How many do you want in your bridal party?
62. Musician[s], always have a backup plan.
63. How long can they stay? [*the whole day is advisable*]
64. How many bridesmaids and ushers?
65. Usher[s], waiters
66. Reception, sit down, or standing: dinner or buffet
67. Reception, with or without children?
68. Reception, morning, afternoon, evening or late evening?
69. Music what song will you use?
70. Who will sing at your wedding?
71. Videography, professional suggested.
72. Gifts and favors.
73. Gift Registrar
74. Wedding Signature Book and pen.
75. Limo, what kind, what's your budget?
76. Book your Limo at least six months in advance.
77. Pick your favorite flowers; can be very costly real or silk?
78. The Cake, start looking now, most caterers won't travel more than twenty-five to fifty miles from the wedding site.
79. Bride and Groom Cake Topper
80. Cake knife and server.
81. Aisle runner.
82. Candle labara.
83. Wishing well, [*assigned a trusted attendant*].
84. What will you use birdseeds, rose petals, or bubbles?
85. Wedding Insurance – *coverage and protection against wedding cancellations.*

86. Parking attendants, if needed.
87. Choosing the caterer, start writing out your menu, the menu will depend on the time of day you will marry.
88. Bridal Shower!
89. Bridal Showers are at the taste of the bride. The bride can dictate what kind of shower she wants. From a girls' only lingerie or personal. Linen, kitchen, couples, barbecue or grilling etc.,
90. We suggest that you ask for what you really want. However, don't get upset when people buy what they want to buy for you whether you ask or not. Therefore, when you are asked what do you like or want, be specific. However, be thankful for all things.
91. Lastly the Surprise Wedding, the perfect celebration for those who don't want a fuss. The spontaneity of a surprise wedding can be a fun and imaginative occasion your guests will hardly forget! For instance, your guest will think that they are arriving for a family reunion, birthday party maybe Christmas or New Year's festivities and instead get to participate in a wonderful event.
92. If this is still too much for you there is always the courthouse. There is absolutely no shame in elopement. It's like practicing abstinence, better safe than sorry.

And you thought it was going to be a piece of cake [*pun intended*]. Yes, the courtship is going to be sweet as cake; so you take courage. Keep your lamp trimmed and burning for the time is drawing nigh. If you decide to call off the wedding, the proper thing to do is return all gifts, including the engagement ring. Include a brief note with each gift you're returning, thanking the person for their thoughtfulness and explaining the wedding will not be taking place. If, unfortunately, you have to cancel your wedding, do not delegate this task; this should be from you or the groom. Take some me time to recuperate. Don't hold any animosity or unforgiveness in your heart.

Remember the only people you should ever want to get "even" with are those who have helped you. – John Honeyfeld

RULE 3:

Just Smile And Keep Your Testimony

"May the God of peace himself sanctify you wholly;
and may your spirit and soul and body be kept sound and blameless
at the coming of our Lord Jesus [יהושע Yahushua] the Christ."
1 Thessalonians 5:23

Christian women are and should always be the classiest, most dignified, honorable, kindhearted and gracious sisters on the face of the earth. We're blessed to be handpicked by God who has graced us with his Holy Spirit, and having given us through the blood of Jesus Christ a Holy reputation of virtue in a wicked, and perverse generation.

This rule reminds me of a church mother who caught me alone in the early stages of my courtship and said very politely to me, "Sister, I would like to speak with you for a moment." She said a few things, I don't remember, but this I certainly remember her saying to me. She said, "blab, blab, blab and Sister now, I don't want you to make *us* [*us meaning the sisters in the church*] ashamed." I'm thinking, "Is there someone else here?

"Make *who* ashamed?" I wanted to look around to see if maybe she was talking to someone else because I felt she didn't know me like that. I didn't want to finish the conversation because she was talking and I was listening with much difficulty, trying to keep my emotions intact and my facial expressions straight, while at the same time, trying really hard not to be disrespectful by finding a reason to excuse myself. I was so carnally insulted! I mean, I felt like I'm good and saved enough, got a good reputation, I'm a grand-mother, and not to mention I had already been married before. I could have said a few mumbling words, but I just smiled.

Thank God for the church mothers that we still have around with seasoned words of wisdom! And I must say, she was quite kind and dignified about how she said it. I'm grateful to God that she did talk to me. In spite of the fact that I didn't like what she said to me, her words of wisdom were good for my soul. Soul food doesn't always taste good but you can believe this it will be good for you if you eat it anyhow. Talking about good soul food, it was seasoned with just enough salt for me to spiritually digest it.

It was just what I needed. What mother was saying to me was, "Daughter, we don't want you to be numbered with the missing in action, named the other [*silly*] woman." I believe the Holy Spirit let her peek into my future, she saw a higher calling on my life, and walked in the bold [*meaning: wise, courageous, valiant, audacious*] grace of a church mother, and gave me a word of advice. Now I know and understand that it was truly out of love and the fact that mother had been around the church long enough to have seen and witness preacher's, teachers, pastors, deacons, choir members, and the like have fallen from grace because of the opposite sex.

It's sad to say most Christian women don't fall into sin outside of church; usually they fall in the Church. Therefore, let me remind you that it's not about age, gender, title, position, education or experiences. It's about keeping a holy reputation of a Christian sister at all times.

When you are courting, you are not courting a title or position, but a person. What am I saying is that titles do not matter. You are still in the flesh; men and women are falling from grace and tainting their honorable reputations every hour of the day. It is perfectly justifiable to wonder, "Who will be left to pass on the baton in Christian courtship?" The church mother just wanted to see the legacy continue by sharing nuggets of wisdom. 1 Thessalonians 4:1-4 "…we beseech you, brethren, and exhort you by the Lord Jesus, that as ye have received of us how ye ought to walk and to please God, so ye would abound more and more,… …That every one of you should know how to possess his vessel in sanctification and honour." She, the church mother, passed the baton and I didn't drop it. To God be the glory!

I didn't know I would one day be a church mother of the highest degree, the first lady, the first mother of the church, but God did. So thank you mother. My head was in the clouds, but my feet were anchored in Jesus. So I'm passing a word of advice to you, my sister, don't become the other woman. Keep your testimony. Don't let your testimony be one of the voluptuous woman, but the virtuous woman.

Some of these Cloud Rules may be hard to the carnal mind but just smile, and keep your testimony. The Holy Spirit has the power to keep you if you want to be kept. He is able to keep you from falling, so you can also say, I've been there and done that. You are fairer than ten thousand. You are one in a million, and if church mothers insist on giving you a little salt be patience you'll understand it better by and by.

Remember, "there hath no temptation taken you but such as is common to man: but God is faithful, who will not suffer you to be tempted above that ye are able; but will with the temptation also make a way to escape, that ye may be able to bear it" [1 Corinthians 10:13]. Maybe more of our sisters would still have their honorable reputations if we had more bold church mothers like the one who approached me.

Everybody doesn't have a natural mother, or maybe even a church mother, so allow these Cloud Rules to encourage you to hold on to your integrity by faith for you haven't seen your best days yet.

It's your time and season to be blessed. Just smile and keep your testimony. Treasure these words of advice my sister. God said you are a good thing, don't drop the ball and become the other women. Keep your testimony and your good name. Remember, "a good name is rather to be chosen than great riches, and loving favour rather than silver and gold" Proverb 22:1.

RULE 4:

Beware Of The Baby Doll Syndrome

"...seven women shall take hold of one man, saying,
we will eat our own bread, and wear our own apparel: only let us be
called by thy name, to take away our reproach." Isaiah 4:1

Our mothers or guardians taught us from infancy how to become loving nurturing mothers and caregivers from the crib. As babies, our mothers who love us dearly placed beautiful soft, cuddly stuffed baby dolls in our bed. Our dolls became our teacher. They provided an outlet for a child's hurt feelings, anger, and other emotions. As we grew older, playing with dolls enabled us to rehearse the roles we hoped to perform after we grow up. The doll has been used as a role model to encourage young girls to grow up to be all that they can or want to be.

Because of the emotional bond formed between girls and their dolls, it has created serious influence on their dysfunctional development of looking for Mr. Right in all the wrong places, including the bed. What is obvious to anyone who has ever seen girls playing with a doll is that whether it is made of cloth, paper, wood, plastic, or some other material, it is more than just a toy. It is a friend, a playmate, and even a confidant with whom little girls share their childhood dream and aspirations with. Having become accustomed to this one-sided, imaginary and fictitious relationship, we grew to know and enjoy our environment with stuff and things that brought us comfort and joy when we were alone and lonely. We learned from little girls how to role-play the family wearing the hat of every member, including, mother, father, and children.

We were always in control, did all the talking, made all the plans and everything always went our way, and things always turned out as we planned. To this day many of our sisters who are all grown up still don't need a man to do anything but give her his name so things can remain as usual. The men don't have to talk, think, work, pay bills, dress himself, or even make a baby, cause we as women have that covered. Just say you will be mine and I will be fine, and I will create my own comfort and joy.

The Baby Doll Syndrome is the fruit of our fallen parent's sin nature. God presented our mother Eve to a full grown man named Adam, not a new born baby. Our society bares the proof of this sin nature fruit by producing babies who want to have babies and not husbands. Our adolescent sisters – barely out of pampers themselves – boldly cry out for someone or something to bring them comfort and joy, by having babies [*as if a toy*]. They want "someone to call their own, someone who will love them unconditionally." Our poor dysfunctional sisters are describing a toy baby doll. The Baby Doll Syndrome is thus perpetuated, teaching our daughters how to be mothers before they became women or wives. Consequently, our sisters are still looking for that personal fictitious one-sided, lopsided relationship that was introduced to them. The cycle repeats itself generation after generation, women looking for unconditional love trying to fill the gap of being lonely and alone with relationship that are filled with empty promises and broken vessels.

Today's modern day sisters are faced with the same dilemma as the women written about in Isaiah 4. Women today say, "Let us all marry you." We will furnish our own food and clothing; only let us be called by your name so that we won't be mocked as old maids." Notice they didn't say so they could have children and be a wife, but for pride sake so that they would have the man's name to cover their shame of being a laughingstock.

My dear sister, get over the Baby Doll Syndrome so you can recognize a godly man and not a baby because if you marry the baby you will always be cleaning up his messes – like holding his hand to help him find a job; feeding him his favorite foods [*not edible food, but things that keep the peace and him pacified in the home*]; paying his phone bills; buying his favorite play toys including cars and trucks, and hats to match. He'll be the man in need, and your role will be the man in deed.

RULE 5:

Choose God's Plan

*"The unmarried woman careth for the things of the Lord,
that she may be holy both in body and in spirit."*
1 Corinthians 7:34

There's a popular movie about a woman who had unfortunately married a man who was a rich abusive infidel entitled *I Can Do Bad All By Myself*. Women love this quotation because it reminds and encourages sisters that they don't have to settle for being in an abusive relationship. The truth is, you can do better, not bad, by yourself, single and unmarried than to subject yourself to being in a bad marriage. Yes, some will also argue that the Bible says it is better to marry than to burn. Well, if you marry the wrong person, it would have been better to burn in the flesh and reap life everlasting, than to marry the wrong person out of the will of God, subjecting yourself to living in hell, and then perhaps end up in hell!

Today's woman seem to have everything but is faced with the fear of whether there are any suitable men left either in or outside of the church. She is still fearful and weeping because loneliness is still one of her greatest unresolved issues. Let me remind you that there is a great difference between being alone and being lonely. Everyone needs personal quiet time [alone time] to focus on the deepest needs of her soul's divine purpose. Even Jesus withdrew himself from crowds, friends, and even his disciples to stay focus on his needs and purpose. Jesus knows the meaning of loneliness, and he desires to be your manfriend. You may be alone sometimes, but he promises you will never have to be lonely with him in your life [Matthew 28:20].

Aloneness is vital for the human being, mind, body, soul, and spirit, but loneliness can be heartbreaking and causes one to feel isolated, unwanted, unneeded and unloved by anyone including God.

Loneliness, on the other hand, is what happens when we are missing real connections and relationships with others. As Christian sisters we want to first remind you Christianity is not just a religion of beliefs. It is a religion of relationships. Saint John 15:1-4 mentions three main relationships:

1. Relationship with the Lord – John 15:1-4
2. Relationship with one another – John 15:12-17
3. Relationship with the world – John 15:18-19

As I write this book, it unfolds more and more as to its purpose. Have you asked yourself why do you want to be married?

1. Is it because you are alone? *or*
2. Is it because you are lonely?

You need to answer those two questions before you say "I do." No one should marry for either reason, because you could easily end up getting married and have a two-fold problem of being alone **and** lonely. I am here to help you think on your feet, and to present sound options for you to consider, like perhaps running if you need to. I want to inform you of the seriousness and gravity of why you should wait on God and allow Him to bless you with a mate. First, don't trust yourself, because man looks on the outward appearance, but God looks on the heart. Not only that, God knows the secrets of the heart of man. "The heart is deceitful above all things, and desperately wicked: who can know it?" [Jeremiah 17:9]

Don't forget you are not the only sister faced with the lopsided world's dilemma of men. Yes, I know it seems so lopsided, men on one side of the world and women on the other. Our world is filled with men. Yes! It is filled with men in the prisons, in the drug and half way houses, in the armed services, third world countries fighting for our freedom, and even on the street corners as if it's their responsibility to hold up the street corners as lamp post.

They are out there. However, Christian sister, this is the real point and the real issue that this book is written: You should not just want a man with flesh and britches, but a man that God desires and has planned for you. That is the bottom line, for a Godly woman to have a Godly man, one who will love her as Christ loves the church. Let's make it a little plainer – a Christian man for a Christian woman. Okay, so I'm repeating myself. It just makes sense for a godly man to be with a godly woman. You want God to choose this man for you because He knows who is His and who is not. There are plenty of men and the marrying kind. Luke Chapter 17 warns that in the last days would be as it was in the days of Noah and Lot, eating drinking, marrying and given in marriage. God desires a man to have his own wife, and a wife to have her own husband.

If you are a believer, then know this, there will be wedding bells until Jesus come, and there will be gavels sounding in the courtroom dissolving marriages until Jesus come. You choose: wedding bells or gavels bells. God's way is the way of peace, not war. God wants you to be happy and if you think differently, that mail came from the devil and not from God's Holy Word. 3 John 1:2 confirms his love and well wishes for you, "Beloved, I wish above all things that thou mayest prosper and be in health, even as thy soul prospereth." Now whose report will you believe? Remember Lot was a godly man, with a wife living in the wicked city of Sodom. God has never left himself without a witness. There are righteous married and unmarried people living everywhere. God has always given his best and he didn't stop at the cross. He has sons after his heart, which loves him, and only wants to please him. They are everywhere in this world in the body of Christ for his use and service.

There are good holy righteous single men living for God in this modern day of Sodom and Gomorrah. They are looking, seeking right now for their soul mate, but you got to have the favor of God to get the best of God.

Abraham was a man of faith, he was faithful to God and God was faithful to him. God is a covenant keeper and he promised that he would withhold no good thing from them who are righteous. Stay faithful to God and if he wants to he will summons an unrighteous man and make him righteous just for you. Remember I said God will do it, meaning he doesn't need your help. You don't have to go out of the family of God, the church, to find him. He will find you.

Men are the pursuers; it's their nature to hunt. Don't take away the chase factor. Many women are so thirsty, that they can't wait on God, and start chasing the men, and when the women catch him, and he skins them like a catfish, then they want to give him back. Amen, somebody!

Let me tell you the most wonderful thing about being chased is when you are caught, and you have those questionable days, you can always remind him, "I didn't pursue you, you pursued me. I didn't ask for your hand in marriage. You asked for my hand in marriage." He'll never be able to say you tricked, manipulated or forced him into marrying you, because you know you were worth the wait. We have included a few tips of what you will face in regards to the rest of the men that's left for your choosing in this wicked and perverted generation. You decide. You chose, "Man's plan" or "God's plan." It's better to be alone in your right mind, than to be beat out of your mind in an abusive relationship. The faithfulness of God's grace brings a far greater reward in waiting for God choice than trying to help God out. Don't forget our sister Sarah, who tried to help God out, and Oh, the mess we are in today!

We have included a few staggering mental and physical health issue statistics in regards to the men and women in our society. We share them with you, not for you to fear, but to avoid and rejoice that you will not be included in this statistic if you truly love God and obey his commands. God is a healer and any mental or physical health issue men or women have no matter how grave, they can be healed and delivered if they believe that Jesus can heal them. There are many witnesses of men and women receiving their healing sometime just by being baptized in the name of Jesus, [Acts 2:38; 8:16; 10:48; and Acts 19:5] and others by the laying on of hands in prayer, asking God to curse the very root of their sicknesses, diseases and problems. These plagues will not come near you, even domestic violence, if you keep his commandments. Diseases are one of the many reasons why Christian women should not be yoked up with unbelievers.

Many unbelievers don't adhere to being in a monogamous relationship, therefore causing grief to many married women. Some unbelieving spouses feel they are grown and what the wife doesn't know won't hurt. So they have girlfriends and may live on the "downlow" i.e., have boyfriends on the side to [*as they say*] keep the spice in their life. We that are intelligent know that multiple sexual partners are ungodly and unhealthy to say the least. I want to share something for you to chew on [*pun intended*]. I was reading a sixth graders sex education pamphlet from school about choosing abstinence until marriage. It said, having pre-marital sex before marriage is like pre-chewed chewing gum. The question was asked, is that what you want to present to your husband?

Something to chew on! Read the statistics on HIV and AIDS in America clearly show that all races are affected, but that ethnic minority's account for a disproportionate number of cases in most states. African Americans are particularly and severely affected by the virus, and relatively high rates of HIV can be found in virtually every sector of the community. The latest Centers for Disease Control report we found on the U.S. epidemic shows that in 2006, 73% of people diagnosed with AIDS were men. Within the African American population, men represent 64% of AIDS cases—64%! Need I say more? You can find more information at your local library or the Internet.

I've heard women say their men came to them saying, "I had a dream and the Lord told me you were my wife." These women often use this as an excuse for putting up with abuse from ungodly men. Please remember that if the LORD told him, the LORD will tell you, too. Your head may be in the clouds but you don't have to be sleep or silly. I have included several profiles of abusers when you see him. Don't try to fix him. In fact, run as fast as you can; don't leave a trace or a phone number. He needs to go back to the factory and let God make him over again. If God don't make him over, you surely won't. Be wise and don't you try. Our men folk have more issues and problems than you can imagine, from immaturity, to health problems, to mental problems, financial problems—must I go on? Nevertheless, they are in high demand in our sin-sick society. Both male and female still come in unbelievable beautifully wrapped packages and when they are unwrapped it's like opening up a Pandora's Box.

God help all of us and our sons and daughters. The only thing we can say or do is pray for God to send his best so you won't end up with the devil's mess. Pray that God will allow him to find you and that you will wait until he does. God doesn't make mistakes. We do. Wait on God before you make a terrible mistake. You as a Christian sister face great odds, and that's a good thing. God always shows out, and shows up when he has small numbers to work with. God can turn it around in your favor. You are already in God's favor, because we know that favor ain't fair. Question is: Can God trust you to wait on him for your blessing?

So don't be silly and gamble with your life or the lives of your unborn children, along with causing unnecessary stress on your family and those who love you. Remember, a man that findeth a wife – *you* – God said is a good thing and the man that marry you will have the favor of God upon his life.

RULE 6:

Read The Handwriting On The Wall

"Many are the plans in a man's heart, but it is the purpose of Yahuah [יהוה] that prevails." Proverb 19:21

This is why we say, write your plans in pencil and give God the eraser.

Many victims of marital abuse often lament, "If only I had seen the hand writing on the wall!" In other words, "I wish I had known the signs of an abuser's personality profile; I would have done differently. The question still remains – how would I know when I am about to become involved with someone who will be abusive?

Many of you may have already seen these signs before, in the relationships of your girlfriends, relatives, co-workers, neighbors and even maybe your mother. For some reason, women can see and recognize all the signs of abuse when it affect others, and not see it when it comes to them. It's like an old saying you can't see the forest for the trees. When you are too close to something it's harder for you to see yourself being abused, and easier for others to see because they are not the party involved. That's why it's good to have at least one honest to goodness true girlfriend, or someone who you trust to tell you the truth. Believe your girlfriend, mother, your children, cousin or whomever you trust to tell you things that you don't want to hear. Remember, they are not in love with your mate you are. For that reason alone, they can be more objective and see things more clearly than you. Maybe that's where the old cliché is so fitting that love is blind.

When your head is in the clouds, you're on a level where you hear no evil, see no evil, and speak no evil. Love truly does cover a multitude of faults. You chose to see only the good in the one you love, especially if you want to be in love. You don't want anything to bust that love bubble, so you cover your eyes, your ears, and you dare listen to your instincts. Yes, your instincts will work, but you will ignore them.

If you have not seen or experience any form of abuse, you are extremely blessed. Stay with God and keep it that way. Obedience is truly better than sacrifice. If you obey the commandments of your heavenly Father, you won't ever have to experience being involved with an abuser. Nevertheless, this information is shared to help you [*my sister*] avoid becoming another victim of abuse or domestic violence.

Here are some Cloud Rules : The person you choose to be in a Christian courtship should:
1. Share the same spiritual convictions – 1 Corinthians 7:39
2. Respect your moral boundaries – 1 Corinthians 6:18
3. Be considerate of you and of others – Philippians 2:4
4. Have a good reputation – Philippians 2:20

I will share with you some indicators that he has strong tendencies toward being an abuser. The more signs a person exhibits, the more likely that the person will batter. In some cases, an abuser may have only a couple of signs that can be recognized. They will try to explain their behavior as signs of love and concern, and you may be flattered at first. As time goes on, the behaviors become more prominent and serve to dominate and control you and the relationship. These behavior sign are seen in people who abuse their partners.

Note: Abuse knows no boundaries, and happens in the world and sad to say, even in the church. This is not because of the will of God, but because of the self will of men, especially in matters of the heart, and in matters of self rule, I can rule myself. Abusers will never see any reasoning for counseling unless; it's to get you some help. Their excuse will be because you need fixing and not them. They will say when you get fixed our problems will be solved.

Don't ignore the signs, domestic violence is a crime! You are not a pet, to jump at commands, a punching bag to relieve anyone of their anxieties, a foot stool, to make anyone feel taller, or a doormat to walk on. The woman was made out of man's side to be equal with him; under his arm to be protected, and near his heart to be loved.

Violence perpetrated upon an intimate partner can take many forms; it can be physically, verbally, emotionally, mentally, sexually, financially, and including restricting one exercise of freedom of religion. This is a constitutional right.

Did you know?
- Every nine seconds a woman is beaten.
- More women are injured by domestic violence than are injured in auto accidents,
- Muggings or by being raped by a stranger.
- Last count, 40% of female homicides occur as a result of domestic violence.
- More than 50% of all homeless women and children are fleeing from domestic violence.
- When a mother is abused, her children are also affected in ways that are both subtle and overt.
- 95% of victims reporting Domestic Violence are women

First domestic violence knows no boundaries. In fact, men who batter come from all economic, social, racial, religious and educational backgrounds. Rarely, is a battering incidence a one-time occurrence. The abuse usually gets worse and happens more frequently over time.

Domestic violence is not just physical abuse:
- Emotional abuse and other controlling behaviors can be just as painful.
- Abuse is used to maintain power and control within a relationship.

Some of the most common forms of manipulation used to maintain power and control are:
- Preventing access to economic resources
- Coercion and threats
- Manipulating children
- Isolation from family and friends
- Intimidation
- Remarks that continually demean one's self-esteem

The lack of paying close attention may someday affect you, those you love, your family, relatives, friends, and neighbors, religious leaders, school officials, the legal system, and our Society at large.

The decisions of a single individual can affect the lives of hundreds of individuals. Individuals who don't even know you, will somehow become involved and affected by one foolish decision. Generational curses, sicknesses, diseases, and idiosyncrasies are passed on in one bad decision in being involved with the wrong mate to your unborn children. We can't choose our parents, siblings or relatives, but thank God he gave us the choice to choose our mate.

Women are the expression of God's love, his kindness and tender mercies. He intended for us to be well provided for and taken care of. The man is to love his wife as Christ loves the Church.

I definitely recommend professional premarital counseling in every case. Notice I said professional counseling. Not your sister, or best friend and etc., a professional counselor who will know how to conduct the sessions. They will ask questions that you will need to consider and they will give advice and recommendations that will prove to be profitable to you if you adhere and follow them before you get to the altar. If your fiancé is not willing to go to premarital counseling when things are great, chances are he won't go to marital counseling when things are not so great.

It's a true saying you can't see the forest for the trees. Sometimes you are too close to something or someone to truly see the signs or the hand writing on the wall in regards to recognizing the profile of an abuser, especially when you believe you are truly in love. Question is, Is he in love with you? Ephesians 5:28-29 teaches, "He that loveth his wife loveth himself. For no man ever yet hated his own flesh; but nourisheth and cherisheth it."

Love truly does cover a multitude of faults. Love chooses to see only the good and makes great sacrifices of tolerance of those that oppose themselves. However, Ephesians 4:32 exhorts, "And be ye kind one to another, tenderhearted, forgiving one another, even as God for Christ's sake hath forgiven you." You want to not only marry the right person for love, but an individual who is kind. Is your mate kindhearted? Don't be blind to the signs.

Beware if your fiancé always insists on getting his way. Sometimes things move too fast with chatting online, talking on the phone, e-mailing, texting. Nothing is more fruitful and fulfilling than a one-on-one, face-to-face old-fashioned relationship. You are learning his ways, his body languages, and his tone of speech. You are learning about his facial expressions, etc. Other forms of communication can take you too fast, and cause you to share too much of your personal information before you can get a chance to really know him.

He's critical and demeaning, always putting you down in private and in public. Ephesians 4:31 Demeaning words even spoken calmly have no place in a loving relationship. Proverb 12:18

He's got a hot temper: Proverb 17:27 A man of discernment is cool of spirit. Shoving, pushing, hitting, always found telling things that are not true, name calling, loud speaking etc., is unacceptable and inexcusable. Ephesians 4:31 – A person with little self-control is hardly ready for marriage. They will be abusive to you, your children, and the family pets. He will constantly make you feel guilty, stupid, treats you like a child, or worthless. He may also constantly check up on your whereabouts, when you get paid, where you bank. He will try to keep you away from your friends and family, exchange phones, drive your car when he has his own, or always ask friends and family to keep an eye on you. He can also accuse you of flirting with others when there is no basis for his doing so. Beware if he makes threats or gives ultimatums, comparing you to others, etc.

Also be aware of him being secretive about your relationship, telling you it's too soon to tell anyone you are engaged. A deliberate attempt to keep the relationship hidden from those who have a right to know about it – spells *trouble*.

On-again, off-again relationship. Proverb 17:17 states: A true companion loves all the time. If you have to keep fixing the relationship, you might do better without it.

Have a history that others have warned you about him, check it out, it may be true! Proverb 15:22 Get all the advice you can, and you will succeed; without it you will fail.

He pressures you for sex. "If you love me, you'll do it. We need to take our relationship to the next level. It's not really sex if there's no intercourse, or penetration." These are all manipulative lines that males [*boys and men*] have used to pressure girls and women into sex. James 3:17; the wisdom from above is first of all chaste. A Christian sister deserve a companion who is morally clean and who respects your chaste sexual boundaries. Don't settle for anything less!

Ignoring or disregarding danger signs in a relationship is like ignoring the warning signals on your car dashboard. It is our Christian duty and responsibility to acknowledge God in all of our ways, including all of our decisions. If we don't have wisdom, we are without excuse. James 1:5 tells us, "If any of you lack wisdom, let him ask of God, that giveth to all men liberally, and upbraideth not; and it shall be given him." No one needs to go into a relationship blindly because they love the Lord. Not only are we responsible to know them that labor among us, it is imperative to know as much as possible about someone you will marry in these last and evil days as you would as someone to check out a car that you want to purchase, a piece of jewelry, or a babysitter for your child.

In case you don't have that someone you can confide in, to be the girlfriend, mother, auntie, or confidant, we have included other unbiased things to consider before you decide to be involved with anyone including an abuser.

Check out their personality traits!

• **Jealousy:** the abuser will say that jealousy is a sign of love. Untrue: Jealousy is a sign of possessiveness and lack of trust. The abuser will question you about who you talk to. You will be accused of flirting, and they will be jealous of time spent with anyone other than themselves. The abuser will call you frequently and unexpectedly drop by at work, etc., and as jealousy progresses, the abuser may refuse to let you work for fear you will meet someone else. In extreme cases they will check car mileage or ask friends to watch you all in the name of love.

• **Controlling Behavior:** The abuser will say they are concerned for your safety; you need to use your time well, or make good decisions. Your lateness from work, store or appointment will make the abuser angry. You will be questioned closely about where you went or who you talked to. You will not be allowed to make personal decisions about the house, personal clothing or attending church. The abuser may keep all the money or even make the partner ask permissions to leave the house or room.

• **Unrealistic Expectations:** An abusive individual will expect his mate to be the perfect lover, parent, friend, etc. to meet all his needs; and if you love him, he will be all you will need. Only God can supply all man's needs, mind, body, soul, and spirit. He will supply all your need according to his riches in glory.

- **Quick Involvement:** You only knew the abuser for less than six months before engagement or marriage. The abuser comes on like a whirlwind, making statements like, "You're the only person I could ever talk to, or I've never felt loved like this by anyone." The abuser will pressure the partner to commit to the relationship in such a way that later the partner may feel guilty or that they are letting the abuser down if they want to slow the relationship down or break it off.
- **Blames Others for Problems:** If the abuser is chronically unemployed, someone is always "doing them wrong" or "out to get them." The abuser makes mistakes and then blames the partner for upsetting them. Whatever goes wrong the abuser will find a way to blame you or you are the reason for anything that goes wrong. You are in a no-win situation.
- **Isolation:** The abusive individual will try to cut the partner off from all sources and resources. If you have male friends you will be called a whore. If you have friends of the same sex they can be called "homosexual." If you are close to family, you are "tied to the apron strings or a daddy's girl." The abuser accuses women supporters of being "trouble makers, or causing trouble." The abuser doesn't want you to have a phone, or even have a phone himself. The abuser may not let the partner use any vehicle, even perhaps your own vehicle, or he will only give you access to one that is not reliable, including tampering with it so that it will only run when he wants it to. The abuser will try to keep the partner from working, going to school, family functions, or even church.
- **Blames others for feelings:** The abuser will tell the partner, "you make me mad, or upset, or you're hurting me by not doing what I want you to do or I can't help being angry. I want to do nice things for you but you make me change my mind every time you don't do what I say." The abuser will use feelings to manipulate the partner such as "You make me happy or you control how I feel."
- **Hypersensitivity:** An abuser is easily insulted and may claim that his feelings are "hurt" when they are really very angry. The abuser takes the slightest setbacks as personal attacks and will rant and rave about the injustice of things that have happened, for instance a traffic ticket or being asked to work overtime or being told

some behavior is annoying. They may be common things that are just a part of living, like blowing your nose or putting on your stockings after putting on your skirt, using a fork instead of a spoon, etc.

• **Threats of Violence:** This could include any threats of physical force meant to control the partner. The abuser will threaten, "I'll slap your mouth off" or I'll break your neck," etc. Non-abusers do not threaten their mates. The abuser will try to excuse threats by saying, "Everybody talk like that."

• **Cruelty to animals or children:** This is a person who punishes animals or children and is insensitive to their pain or suffering. The abuser may expect children to be capable of doing things beyond their ability. The abuser may tease until they cry. The abuser may not want children to eat at the table or make them stay in their room all evening while the abuser is home.

• **Playful Use of Force in Sex:** This kind of person may like to throw the partner down and hold them down during sex. The abuser may want to act out fantasies during sex where the partner is helpless. Trying to influence the idea of rape as exciting. The abuser show little concern about whether the partner wants to have sex and uses sulking or anger to manipulate them into compliance. The abuser may start having sex without the consent of the partner while the partner is sleeping or demand sex when the partner is tired or ill etc.

• **Verbal Abuse:** The abuser will say things that are meant to be cruel and hurtful. This can be seen when the abuser degrades the partner, cursing them, running down the partner's accomplishments. The abuser will tell the partner that they are stupid and unable to function without them. This may involve waking the partner up in the middle of the night to verbally abuse them or not letting them go to sleep. I give my beloved sweet sleep… [Psalm 127:2]

• **Rigid Sex Roles:** The abuser expects a woman to serve the abuser. The abuser may say that the woman must stay at home, that the partner must obey in all things, even things that are criminal in nature. The abuser will see the female gender as inferior to males, responsible for menial tasks, stupid and unable to be a whole person without a relationship.

• **Dr. Jekyll and Mr. Hyde personality:** Many partners are confused by the abuser's sudden change in mood. The partner may think that the abuser has some special mental problem because one minute the abuser is nice and the next minute the abuser's exploding. Explosiveness and moodiness are typical of people who abuse their partners. These behaviors are related to other characteristics like hypersensitivity.

• **Past physical violence:** The abuser has hit partners in the past, but "they made me do it." You may hear from the abuser's relatives or ex-spouse/partner that the person is abusive. The abuser will abuse any partner if they stay long enough for the violence to begin. Situational circumstances do not make a person resort to violence. If the husband is not pleased to stay let him leave...[1 Corinthians 7:15]

• **Breaking or striking objects:** This behavior [*breaking cherished possessions*] is used as a punishment, but is equally designed to terrorize the partner into submission.

• **Using force during an argument:** Examples of this are kicking, punching, slapping, hair-pulling, pinching, biting, stomping, poking, spitting and any means of physically restraining the partner from leaving a room. The abuser may hold the partner against her will, and say "you're going to listen to me!" Weapons of choice are also often involved as well.

A true man or woman that has been born again of God will not and should not have any of these ungodly characteristics. "And such were some of you..." [1 Corinthians 6:11]. He will be a new creation, old things are passed away and behold all things become new [2 Corinthians 5:17]. Old characteristics bring shame and disgrace upon the church of the living God and his people.

We are in this world but are not of this world. We are pilgrims just passing through, and we are not to ignorantly choose to participate in any relationship that does not bring honor or glory to our heavenly Father. Just as in the beginning our parents [*Adam and Eve*] were given choices, to obey or not to obey, to live or to die. They chose death, and passed on that sin nature to their offspring. Men and women are choosing daily dysfunctional lifestyles that only bring shame, disappointment, grief, etc.

It is also true that domestic violence is a crime not only against women but men as well. There are plenty of women who are abusive towards men and towards their husbands. Men are daily filing Order of Protection Petitions against their female abuser. Proverb 30:21-23

I spoke with a young man who was in a relationship with a woman who slapped him and then wanted to make love—oh excuse me—have sex. There are sister's out there who fall in the above mentioned abuse category. There are women who feel that if the man doesn't fight them, he doesn't love them. If you are a Christian woman who is overbearing, domineering, and odious there is help for you. Remember your mother Eve. Put your past behind you, seek counseling and pray to God for help in this area of dysfunction. Keep reading this book there is a blessing waiting for you.

Take note! If several different people tell you the same thing including reading this book then you have been advised; however, the decision and choice is still yours. Do yourself a favor and Read the Handwriting on the Wall.

It's funny how we fuss over stuff and things that we put way too much value in. Things that will rust and fade away, yet when it come to our bodies, our mind and our soul we seem to be clueless as to how much we are worth as a person and to our Creator. Someone said, measure wealth not by the things you have, but by the things you have for which you would not take money. As you seriously take into consideration your worth, we have listed a few types of characters to avoid:

- **The Disguiser Is a user:** Threatens you that if you do not have sex, he will find someone who will.
- **The Conceited:** You're blessed to have me.
- **The Sicko:** Let me tie you up in knots. If you do your life will be a nightmare
- **The Sluggard:** Mr. Lazy Bones. My day is spent at your beckoning call; you will work for the both of you. The sure procrastinator and dreamer.
- **The Gift Giver:** Always putting you in a guilt bag for everything he does for you and gives you; you will always be indebted. You will always give more than you receive.
- **The Snake:** always tell half-truths, smooth as butter, never ever trust, forgive and let go.
- **The Abuser:** You made me angry, I wanted to do right by you, but you made me change my mind.

Breaking Off The Engagement

You may be a sister who just got engaged because it was the first time you were proposed to, or maybe you didn't want to be left out because all your friends are getting married. Perhaps your family members are in love with him but you are not; if so, you are a people pleaser. Deep inside you are uncomfortable and have your doubts. Do you want to slow things down or rethink the situation? Here are some tips:

- **Be courageous:** It takes courage to speak up when a relationship needs more time. Standing up for yourself is healthy. "A prudent man foreseeth the evil, and hideth himself: but the simple pass on, and are punished" Proverb 22:3. Setting the pace enables you to establish firm boundaries as to what you will and what you will not tolerate in a relationship, and later, in a marriage.
- **Be fair:** If you were on the other end of the dissolution, how would you want to be treated? Does the individual deserve more than a brief email, text or voicemail with the not-so-good news? Treat others as you want to be treated. [Matthew 7:12]
- **Choose the right setting:** Decide how and where. Should you write a letter, or have a face-to-face discussion? Much depends upon the circumstances. You should not meet in any setting where your safety would be put in jeopardy, nor would it be wise to be in any isolated area where wrong desires could be stirred. "For this is the will of God, even your sanctification, that ye should abstain from fornication: That every one of you should know how to possess his vessel in sanctification and honour" [1 Thessalonians 4:3-4].
- **Speak truthfully,** honestly about why you know the relationship is not of God. Make talking points and stick to viewpoint statements.
- **Be willing to listen:** Is there something you've misunderstood about the situation? Do not allow yourself to be manipulated by clever words, however; but be reasonable and consider all the facts. "Be swift to hear, slow to speak, slow to wrath: For the wrath of man worketh not the righteousness of God" James 1:19-20.

For a good source of information, we recommend you to go to your local library, internet and other resources to find out, what is Domestic Violence?

What is the Batterer Behavior? Find information on *The Profile of an Abuser, and the Cycles of Violence.* We say again... Write your plans in pencil and give GOD the eraser!

RULE 7:

Risk Love

The Dilemma

"God has not given us the spirit of fear, but of power,
and of love and of a sound mind." 2 Timothy 1:7

Many years ago, I saved this poem, "The Dilemma," written by an unknown author, from a newspaper clipping. I don't remember why it interested me so or why I kept it so long until I found myself in a dilemma. I had been proposed to and it was hard for me to say the words, I love you. It's easy to say the words, but do you really mean it? As a mature woman who had been married for over twenty-five years in her first marriage, hearing those words was an issue for me. To me love is not just what you say, but what you say and do. I was in a dilemma:

How can I marry someone when I am struggling with the words "I love you?" Being what you would call an old-school girl, I had never considered marrying for stuff and things, but I always believed that one should marry for love. I really, really liked this man, but could I truly love him? After all the things I've been through, is it really possible for me to love him? Saying I love you, was like speaking a foreign language. Should I marry for the sake of being married again, for security, or stuff and things?

Then this poem that I had saved for years dropped in my spirit. I search high and low to find this poem. I knew it was my confirmation from God. The words I love you, were just words, they had no meaning until I was ready to let down my walls, put out my old garbage of past hurt and pain on the curb, and allow myself to love and be loved. Finally, I let my hair down, literally, and along came the love bug and escorted me into the clouds of love. I allowed myself to be loved, and gave myself permission to fall in love. It proved to be a wonderful risk worth taking. The man I liked so much became so easy to love. I share this poem with you just in case you find that you're in a dilemma and afraid to risk loving for the first time, or risk loving again!

The Dilemma
[author unknown]

To laugh is to risk appearing a fool.
To weep is to risk appearing sentimental.
To reach out for another is to risk involvement.
To expose feelings is to risk rejection.
To place your dreams before the crowd is to risk ridicule.
To love is to risk not being loved in return.
To go forward in the face of overwhelming odds is to risk failure.
But risks must be taken because the greatest hazard in life
   is to risk nothing.
The person who risks nothing does nothing, has nothing, is nothing.
He may avoid suffering and sorrow, but he cannot learn, feel, change,
   grow or love.
Chained by his certitudes, he is a slave.
He has forfeited his freedom.
Only a person who takes risks is free.

Love is worth the risk, because it's better to experience loving and being love if only but once in your life. Be blessed my sister. You are not crazy for loving and allowing yourself to be loved. In fact, use the Word of God as your guide and allow yourself to do just that. If you keep the advice of the Cloud Rules, you can be sure that God will keep you from falling.

Eye Openers

There was a survey conducted in the 90s by a writer for *Psychology Today* who wrote eight basic expectations of both sexes.

They were:

1. Affection
2. Communication
3. Honesty
4. Compatibility
5. Unconditional Acceptance
6. Attractiveness
7. Enthusiasm
8. Intelligence

Sad to note this, but where is Love? I guess someone would answer what's love got to do with it? Well, let's see? What would keep you together if all the above mentioned was no longer an ingredient in your marriage what would keep you from getting divorced? Love would do it.

Love: without it, what else matters? "My little children, let us not love in word, neither in tongue; but in deed and in truth" 1 John 3:18. "Charity never faileth" 1 Corinthians 13:8.

There are many things people say they love: flowers, candy, peanuts, pizza, soap operas, movies, walking etc., but these strong cravings are for one's own pleasure, and should not be confused with real love. These feelings come and go with gratification. How to differentiate is simple: lust takes and has no conscience while love gives and holds no ills.

Real love is the benevolent, loyal, sacrificial concern one has for another. Love is patient and kind. Love is not jealous or boastful. It is not arrogant or rude. Love does not insist on its own way, it is not irritable or resentful. It does not rejoice at wrong, but rejoices in the right. Love bears all things, believes all things, hopes all things, endures all things. Love never ends. It seeks to serve others and is at its best service when the need is the greatest. Love is not a feeling even though it feels great to be in love. It's not what one says, but the proof is in what one does. When a man loves a woman, he proves it by what he says and does. If he tells her that he loves her, he will prove it and marry her.

God is the author of marriage. He intended for it to be a happy and fulfilling experience in a person's life. Having a happy marriage should be every couple's goal. We are finite creatures of various temperaments of strengths and weaknesses. God's divine purpose was for man and woman to be equally yoked not unequally [*unalike, lopsided, off-balance, etc.*], yoked. God instituted marriage between two people who have committed themselves in holy matrimony to live in unity and harmony for all their natural lives. Therefore, if you have another reason or purpose for marrying, you will have to live with the consequences of being unequally yoked.

Now, for those of you who are getting married because you truly love your mate then these Eye Opener Rules, as many as it seems, in reality are just a few topics of discussion that should be shared. First, we must admit to ourselves that we are not perfect creatures, and everyone has idiosyncrasies, meaning having characteristics that are odd, strange, eccentric, peculiar to themselves. As you endeavor to become one, you will have to work through a multitude of subjects to help in the process of becoming acquainted with your soon-to-be spouse. You must accept the fact that all humans reflect both strength and weaknesses including you and your soul mate. Therefore, the sooner you face the fact that anyone you marry will have weaknesses to which you must adjust, especially if you are older and experienced, the happier you will be. You will certainly have more baggage. Therefore, the quicker you can move on to the business of adjusting to your partner, the less time you will waste reaching your goal to having a happy Godly marriage.

Go into your marriage with your **eyes wide open**. It matters not if you are getting married for the first time or remarrying. It is a wise individual who will seek a partner to which they will have much in common, naturally and spiritually [*compatibility*]. Never take for granted or assume anything that has not been discussed. Just because he is a believer doesn't mean that you have the same goals or want the same things. You may be on the same page spiritually, but equally importantly is being on the same page naturally. If you don't consider this, you will be going into a marriage with your head in the sand. Having your *Cloud Rules* handbook while your head is in the clouds is a much better atmosphere. It will help you to see before you see.

Now is the time to ask and answer anything you want to know about your soon-to-be spouse. After reading the list of questions, write down your own and have a great time getting acquainted with your new love. Remember marriage is 24/7, and being a Christian is 24/7. This is not a lifestyle of convenience when it's convenient, but a promise to keep when it's not convenient. Your wedding vows will remind you that you will have to be committed to live a life of subjection and benevolence all day every day, for better and worst of times.

This is why we have included the Read the Handwriting on the Wall Rule. No wife is to be offended into subjection but loved into submission. "The husband is the head of the wife; even as Christ is the head of the church… and just as the church is subject unto Christ, so let the wives be to their own husbands…Husbands are to love their wives as their own bodies. He that loveth his wife loveth himself." The Bible goes on to say that no man ever yet hated his own flesh; but nourisheth and cherisheth it. Ephesians 5:31 explains, "For this cause shall a man leave his father and mother, and shall be joined unto his wife, and they two shall be one flesh." Ephesians 5:33 also goes on to say a man is to "so love his wife even as himself; and the wife see that she reverence her husband." If wives are to be chastised by anyone, it is God who will do the chastisements, because we belong to him, and bought with a price by the blood of Jesus Christ. Don't ever forget who and whose you are. Husbands and wives are partners for Christ.

These Eye Opener Rules were inspired because of the last days in which we live in. Men are lovers of themselves. This is why we feel that all the silly women will be a part of that great falling away, from men who will come into the church and lead them out captive. These men will be designer demons, whose assignment will be to take you out and wreck havoc of your souls. "For of this sort are they which creep into houses, and lead captive silly women laden with sins, led away with divers lusts" 2 Timothy 3:6. We have included a multitude of funny, interesting and serious topics for you to discuss during your courtship. Some of these same subject matters have caused many divorces simply because the subject never was discussed before the "I do's." These questions include personal data about your mate, favorites, pets, children, family, careers, finances and church attendances, etc. If you find yourself paying his bills, or giving him loans before marriage, put it in writing terms and conditions and date it. If it was a gift, don't be an Indian giver. Don't take anything for granted. There's an old saying, how you start out is usually how you will end up.

Don't assume that your mate knows what you are thinking or feeling. He is not God and is not a mind reader. Don't put that kind of pressure or confidence in your mate. God gave you a mouth to express your feeling and thoughts to your soul mate. Being in love will give you a false sense of security that your soul mate can read your mind. Don't be deceived. Talk while he will listen. Talk about likes and dislikes. You'll be surprise of the things he likes and/or dislikes.

Take this valuable courtship time to get to know your mate. Whatever you do, don't ask all these questions in the same day. Instead, feed them little by little, one question at a time. Rome wasn't built in a day; neither are great and wonderful relationships.

Take some of these questions and make it a game. Have a few friends over for a fish fry or barbecue. Have a couple's night of clean Christian fun. Put the questions in a fish bowl or cookie jar. You be creative. Take these questions or any variation you like and play a game. How well do you know your mate? The object of the game is honesty. If it's too personal or the person don't want to answer it, the individual will say I pass, and put the question back in the bowl. They will skip a turn, come back and pick another question, and keep playing the game. You don't want to set your mate up to tell something that is not true. Do not put the asked questions back in the bowl. Have a note pad with you, and write down the questions your mate passes on. You may want to ask these questions again at another time, in private or at another's couple's night. Pay close attention to questions that really mean something to you until you get the answer that satisfies you.

Just Talk About It!

Here are a few revealing questions to find out how compatible you are, naturally and spiritually. Many of these questions may or may not apply to you personally depending on age, experience and level of maturity, both naturally and spiritually. However, in time they may all be applicable after marriage.

Here's an example: You may be in love with someone who do not care for children, and if you love children and want them that will be a problem, and vice versa. **Questions to talk about:**

- Can they have children? Can you have children? Don't let it be a surprise if you can't.
- Do you want children?
- Does he want children?
- Does he like or love children?
- What is their opinion on abortion?
- How many children? Is that an option?
- How do he feel about adoption, foster parenting, grandchildren, or extended families?
- Why do you want to be married?
- What are your reasons for marrying?
- Why are you getting married?
- What is the difference between being alone, and being lonely?

- What about sex? *You may marry someone who wants it 24/7 and you may be fine with once a week or vice versa.*
- How does he feel about your pastor or his pastor?
- How does he feel about adoption of your children?
- How will the bills be paid? And who will be responsible for what?
- How do you or your mate feel about relatives or extended family members moving in?
- How does he feel about paying tithes and giving offering?
- How does he feel about church attendance, particularly week nights or Sunday nights?
- How important or unimportant are these verses… Acts 1:8 and Acts 2:38?
- How often does he think a Christian should pray? weekly, daily, etc.?
- Does he think he should have a set prayer time, or pray when they feel the spirit of prayer?
- What's important how long one prays, or how often one prays?
- How does he feel about your position in the church?
- Does he own a Bible?
- If he was asked to offer prayer over supper, what scripture would he use?
- If he could use only one scripture in the Bible leading someone to salvation what would it be? without using Saint John 3:16
- How does he feel about volunteer services? Would you be free to do things without pay?
- What if God called you in the ministry?
- Would he hinder your ministry?
- Do you have a calling on your life? Does he have a problem accepting your calling?
- Does he have an aught against anyone?
- How does he feel about obeying leadership?
- Does he love God?
- Does he know who God is?
- Who is God?
- Does he have God in his life?
- How do you know he has God in his life?
- Has your partner been married before? If so, how many times?
- Where was he divorced, what city and state? Why did he get a divorce?
- Is he a U.S. Citizen?

- Does he have children? If so, how many? Does he know their birthdays?
- How old are his children? What are their birth dates?
- Is their mother living?
- Is she their natural, adoptive, stepmother, godmother, foster, play mother, etc?
- In one word how would he describe his relationship with his mother?
- Describe his relationship with his children in one sentence?
- When was the last time he told his mother I love you?
- What is his definition of love?
- Is it better to marry for love or for being in love?
- How long should children sleep in the same bed with their parents?
- Should anyone get married because they got pregnant?
- Should fathers have a say in their children being breast feed?
- How do you feel about mother's who breast feed longer than a year?
- What role will you play as a stepparent?
- Does he pay child support?
- How long will he have to pay child support?
- What are his feelings/knowledge on domestic violence?
- What are his priorities? Is God at the head of his list?
- What will be your stand on loaning money to family, friends or parents?
- Does he pay bills for his relatives, parents or children?
- Will that continue after marriage?
- Who will pay the family bills?
- Does he have a public library card?
- What municipality do you look under to find state phone numbers?
- What pages yellow, green, blue, etc?
- When was the last time he had a dental exam?
- When was the last time he had an eye exam?
- Has he ever suffered mental illness?
- Does he believe in bankruptcy?
- Has he ever filed for bankruptcy?
- What are his goals, plans, visions or ambition in life?
- Is it in his head, or is it written down?
- Who knows his goals, etc?
- How close is he in reaching his goals?
- Does he think goals are important or just one of life's option?

- What is his total debt?
- If he was fired today, how long could he pay his bills rent/mortgage without working?
- How often does he read his Bible?
- What is his favorite Bible verse? Why?
- How often do you think you should read your Bible?
- How important is Bible reading?
- Does he believe the whole Bible to be true?
- What is his faith? Why?
- Does he think all Christians are alike?
- What is a Christian?
- What does he believe?
- Does he believe Jesus and God is the same person?
- Does he believe in Jesus?
- Does he believe Jesus is God?
- Is Jesus God?
- Can he prove Jesus is God?
- Is Jesus alive? How does he know Jesus is alive?
- How can a person be saved?
- What is the rapture?
- Is he looking forward to the rapture?
- Who will be in the rapture?
- Is he a born again Christian?
- How does he know he is a born again Christian?
- Should born again Christians marry unbelievers?
- Is it wrong for Christian women to marry non-Christian men or vice versa?
- Will your spouse have to work? Even if you are already working.
- Does he think it's wrong to marry for any other reason besides love?
- Does he think it's ok to marry for any other reason besides love?
- Should husbands and wives sleep in the same bed every night, even when upset?
- Does he think it's wrong for husbands and wives to sleep in separate beds?
- How does he feel about eating together as a family?
- Should meals be eaten together or separately?
- Does he attend Sunday School?
- Does he think it's important to attend Sunday School?

- How is his credit?
- Does he have a problem with a wife making more money than him?
- What is his highest level of education?
- If he found out that his fiancé told you an untruth would you call off the engagement?
- For what reason[s] would he call off the engagement?
- Would he seek counseling before calling off the engagement?
- What does an engagement ring mean to him?
- Will he be able to purchase a home or will you have to live with relatives?
- Does he have a saving account?
- Do you have a habit of savings?
- Is there anything we should discuss before we get married?
- What is his family's medical history/health issues?
- Does he take medicine, and why?
- Does he have a J.O.B.?
- What is his work history?
- What was the first physical thing that attracted him to you?
- If that attraction was lost, damaged, injured, how would he handle it? Example: Lost limb.
- How much would he be willing to sacrifice for your family, friends or parents?
- Who would come first, and why?
- How soon does he want to start a family?
- Does he already have a name for the first born? Is it up for discussion?
- How does he feel about continued education?
- Where are we going to live? Your house, my house, or momma's house?
- How does he feel about pets?
- Does he have any pets? What are they?
- Does he sleep with his pets?
- Does he intend to continue to sleep with his pets after marriage?
- What time does he go to bed?
- Does he expect his spouse to go to bed at the same time?
- Does he have to sleep with the light, radio or television on?
- How long does he feel you should be physically fit?
- How does he feel about taking family pictures?
- How does he feel about tattoos?

- Does he have allergies?
- Can he fix a flat tire?
- Does he take vacations? How often?
- What are his family traditions?
- What will be our family traditions?
- Does he believe in family prayer?
- Does he believe in celebrating holidays?
- How does he celebrate holidays?
- Where does he celebrate his holidays?
- How does he feel about husbands and wives taking separate vacations?
- Does he think it's more important for fathers to work vs. vacation time with family?
- Does he believe in budgeting?
- How will we budget our family funds?
- Does he believe in celebrating birthdays, anniversaries?
- Does he feel housewives should be given personal funds besides funds to run the house? How often? How much?
- Is he romantic?
- What was the last romantic gesture he performed?
- What does he call cheap?
- Define a cheap person.
- Is he a spend thrift?
- Does he believe you should confess your sins, or *tell a friend*?
- How does he feel about a spouse having a secret bank account?
- Should he pay his bills before his tithes or vice versa? Why?
- Does he have phobias?
- Should career changes be a family discussion?
- Who's money is it: his, her or ours?
- If the wife is working and should become pregnant how long is she expected to work?
- What are his feelings regarding her returning to work after the baby is born?
- Is it necessary to feel like he runs the house?
- What are his feelings regarding children, relatives, friends, in-laws, out-laws, etc.?
- What are his feelings regarding church attendance, tithes and offerings, positions held in church, etc.?

- What are his feelings regarding spending money, loaning money, saving money, joint account/personal account?
- What are his feelings regarding family counseling, children, personal, marriage, etc.?
- Would he have a problem with family counseling?
- How does he feel about caring for aging parents?
- How old is he?

You get the idea! I thought I would save some questions for you. They say love is blind, and your head may be in the clouds, but don't be silly. After you talk about something lovingly to your partner, if there is no immediate resolve, commit the matter to God for directions. You must resist all mental fantasies of perfection here on earth and pray for yourself and your partner, for the strengthening of your weaknesses. Be reminded that God loves you and only wants the best for you. He says, I know the thoughts that I think towards you, thoughts of peace and not of evil to give you an expected end. You need to talk about every possible subject to become acquainted with your mate in other relevant areas. He may not like or even want to answer the questions, but if he loves you he will. If he truly love you and is marrying you for love, he will answer any and all questions without reservation.

Unequally Yoked

Given all the issues the Eye Opener questions raise, you can now see why is it important to believe God's word in regards to being unequally yoked. There is plenty of adjusting to do even with believers marry believers. That's why we trust the Word of God that has our best interest in mind: "For I know the thoughts that I think toward you, saith the Lord, thoughts of peace, and not of evil, to give you an expected end" Jeremiah 29:11. Man's heart is "desperately wicked" Jeremiah 17:9. "Man looks on the outward appearance but God looks on the heart. He made the heart; does he not know it?"

"Let the husband render unto the wife due benevolence: and likewise also the wife unto the husband. The wife hath not power of her own body, but the husband: and likewise also the husband hath not power of his own body, but the wife. Defraud ye not one the other, except it be with consent for a time, that ye may give yourselves to fasting and prayer; and come together again, that Satan tempt you not for your incontinency" [*meaning-lacking self-restraint in regard to sexual desires*] 1 Corinthians 7:3-5.

This will not be a hard thing to do when you love each other and have much in common naturally and spiritually; in fact, it will be a joy. This is one of God's ways for marriage to be a life of pleasure and not a life of drudgery. Is this the person you want to love for life? Just as Christ is married to the Church, you will be married to an individual who God commands to love you as Christ loves the church. The married life of spirit-filled believers has specific godly rules to live by. [Ephesians 5:22-31].

God gave Eve a man of great wealth and worth. He did not give our mother an infidel, and he doesn't want her daughters marrying infidels. God is still a God of great loving-kindness and tender mercies. Think about how good God has been to you, then and now and then thank God he gives you his Word to help you enter marriage with your eyes wide open.

RULE 8:

You Are Worth The Wait!

"There be three things which are too wonderful for me,
yea, four which I know not: The way of an eagle in the air;
the way of a serpent upon a rock; the way of a ship in the midst of the sea;
and the way of a man with a maid." Proverb 30:18-19

Have you ever asked yourself how much are you worth? I want to share a true conversation that I had in the store one day as I was standing behind a man in line. This man was making a purchase and while interacting with the cashier, I noticed he dropped a penny. I said to the man, excuse me, mister, you dropped a penny. He said to me in a jovial way, "Thank you, but you could have waited until I left and picked it up and kept it for yourself." I laughed and said "It wasn't worth it being a penny and all." Then he said to me, "Everybody has a price and can be bought if the price is right." I said, "Not for that amount." Then I thought about what I had said and corrected my statement and said emphatically, "Not for any amount."

You know how those store lines are sometimes, we had a few more minutes, and he laughed and proceeded to tell me of a story he was reminded of about a man and a woman in a bar. It went like this: there was a woman at the bar drinking, and a man came up to her and said, "If I gave you a million dollars would you have sex with me?" The woman answered, "Yes." Then the man said, "Well, I don't have a million dollars, but how much will you have sex with me for?" The woman said, quite insulted, "What do you think I am?" The man said, "We have already established that part, I just want to know, what is your price?" Wow! That was a stomach punch. I never forgot that story, and it seemed appropriate to open this chapter.

Don't be deceived. Age, money, education, titles, experience, clout or such cannot immune you from the advances of a man when his heart is set on getting what he wants. The only shield you will have is the power of God working in your life. The man just wants to know what your price is. "Abstain from all appearance of evil. And the very God of peace sanctify you wholly; and I pray God your whole spirit and soul and body be preserved blameless unto the coming of our Lord Jesus Christ" [1 ThesselonIANS 5:22-23]. You often times hear people say they don't care what people say about them. Well you should care, because you represent God. What? Know you not that your body is the temple of the Holy Ghost?

Watch yourself. I know you're feeling pretty good round about now. The Holy Spirit is ministering. Let him have his way! You can trust God just a little while longer. It's not as long as it has been. It will be worth the wait. Your presence and womanly personage is a handwritten speech of a mighty God. You are an exquisite portrait, a walking thesaurus of everything lovely and divine. God is speaking, when he made you. We as women can never forget the mother of all living, Mother Eve. She gave us the first punch in the stomach because she didn't understand her worth either.

The question again is how much are you worth? If you don't know, your lifestyle may have already established that part for you. Someone said it ain't what people call you, but it's what you answer too. Now what is your price? Or the price you are willing to pay? Remember, you can't use your wages of sin to buy your way into heaven; we have to live by God's rules to be at peace with him. For ye are bought with a price; therefore glorify God in your body, and in your spirit, which are God's. God is concerned about our body, soul, and spirit. What about you?

Many feel we can do anything with our bodies and give only our heart to God. One without the other is only deception. If your heart truly loves God you will seek to please him [*wholly*] which includes your body. Remember the story of the seven women who wanted to marry one man; they were all concerned about their bodily appearance and how it displeased God. If you love your husband with your heart, do you want to please him with your body? Of course, you will be concerned with how you look, how you dress, how you smell, including your morning breath. You will be concerned about the clothes you wear, in the day and in the evening. You will be concerned with your grooming from your head to your toes, how you walk, how you talk, and how you present yourself to others, in his presence or in the absence of his presence, because you are his good thing, you will represent him. All of these examples are not spiritual but natural and relative to the human body and its features.

The Apostle Paul listed a number of sinful people who will not inherit a place in the kingdom of God. This list was a reminder to the Corinthians of what they had been prior to God's saving Grace in their lives. 1 Corinthians 6:9 "Know ye not that the unrighteous shall not inherit the kingdom of God? Be not deceived; neither fornicators, nor idolaters, nor adulterers, nor effeminate, nor abusers of themselves with mankind, nor thieves, nor covetous, nor drunkards, nor revilers, nor extortioners, shall inherit the kingdom of God." Verse 11 "And such were some of you; but ye are washed, but ye are sanctified, but ye are justified in the name of the Lord Jesus, and by the Spirit of our God." Verse 15, "Know ye not that your bodies are the members of Christ? Shall I then take the members of Christ, and make them the members of an harlot? God forbid." Verse 18 "Flee fornication. Every sin that a man doeth is without the body; but he that commiteth fornication sinneth against his own body."

"What? know ye not that your body is the temple of the Holy Ghost which is in you, which ye have of God, and ye are not your own?" [1 Corinthians 6:19]. A good wife never seeks to embarrass her husband by her physical [bodily] appearance. How much more should we as Christian women who are the physical and spiritual bride of Jesus Christ be concerned with our bodily appearance, presence and behavior?

Can you imagine how embarrassed God must be by the bodily appearance of his so called bride? We say we are Christian, which means Christ like, yet, we present ourselves to the world as harlots by the way we look, walk, talk, dress, act, smell, and etc. all bodily [physical] attraction.
—*Hmmmmmm.*

Looking for Mr. Right is Wrong!

"Whoso findeth a wife findeth a good thing,
and obtaineth favour of Yahuah [יהוה]." Proverb 18:22

Remember, God had Adam to name all the living breathing creatures, and he couldn't find one to relate or mate with. God saw Adam's need, before the woman was even created. Woman was created because the man was alone. You are worth the wait, just as Adam waited for Eve. Steve, Larry, Michael [*or whatever his name is*] can wait for you.

I read something that said I always know God won't give me more than I can handle but there are times I wish he didn't trust me so much. Naturally, we want to make choices without consulting anyone including God. These are the choices we know deep inside are chance decisions without good or sound judgment. A test that God gives us is not to take us out, but to take us further and bring us closer to him. He tests us because he trusts his Spirit within us. We cannot be trusted; courtship can be considered your probationary season. You are not the mother of Jesus; this engagement does not mean you are his wife.

Don't you understand yet, that you are so wanted that your man will yearn for your love as King Solomon did the Shulamite woman? He will look for you, because there is no other creature in the world that can satisfy his longings. Women underestimate their worth and give it away [*their body that is*] for a #3, hamburger, fries and pop. Their fifteen minute sexual experience was the same amount of time it took to super size their drink, waiting in the fast food drive in. You can wait and you are worth waiting for. Remember, all true Christian women live by the same rule as in Philippians 3:16. Let us [*my Christian sisters*] walk by the same rule, let us mind the same thing.

RULE 9:

Be A Virtuous Woman

Who can find a virtuous woman?
For her price is far above rubies.
Proverb 31:1

A virtuous woman is precious and priceless in the sight of God. Question is, who can find such a woman? "The heart of her husband doth safely trust in her, so that he shall have no need of spoil. She will do him good and not evil all the days of her life. She openeth her mouth with wisdom; and in her tongue is the law of kindness. She looketh well to the ways of her household, and eateth not the bread of idleness. Her children arise up, and call her blessed; her husband also, and he praiseth her." The worth of a virtuous married woman to her husband, family, society and the church is invaluable and beyond worldly wealth. The biblical virtuous woman is not just one particular woman but a superb portrait of ideal womanhood, one with outstanding abilities, and incredible, incalculable worth!

Her value is priceless! Education, family roots, wealth, or status in life cannot purchase this value. It is impossible to put a value on the worth of a virtuous woman, the scripture testifies, for her worth is above the value of rubies. Of all the roles, duties and responsibilities women have, none are more valuable or important than the role of a mother or wife in the home.

The Virtuous Woman
Proverb 31

Her attributes are described in the bible.

- She is loyal [verse 11]
- She is a home maker [chapter 31]
- She is hard to find [*a rare gem,* verse 10]
- She is precious [Proverb 31:10]
- She has inner beauty [*heart attractions* 31:30; 1 Peter 3:4]
- She works with her hands [*a lovely life producing loving words*]
- She is right with God [Proverb 31:30]
- She abides in the home [Proverb 31:27]
- She does her husband good [Proverb 31:12]
- She is resting at night so she can awake early [Proverb 31:15]
- She blesses her family [Proverb 31:28]
- She lives by love [Proverb 31:20]

A Voluptuous Woman
"Such is the way of an adulterous woman;
she eateth, and wipeth her mouth, and saith,
I have done no wickedness" Proverb 30:20

- She is lewd [Proverb 6:24; 2:17]
- She is a home breaker [Proverb Chapter 7]
- She is easy to find [Proverb 7:10-12]
- She is cheap [Proverb 30:20]
- She has outer beauty [Proverb 6:25]
- She works with her mouth [*lively lips but no life,* Proverb 21:9, 19; 25:24]
- She is religious [Proverb 7:14]
- She work outside the home [Proverb 7:11-12]
- She does her husband nothing but harm [Proverb 2:17]
- She is on the loose [*during the day and*] at night [Proverb 7:9, 18]
- She lives by lust [Proverb 7:10].

S.O.S.
"…ye have us for an ensample" Philippians 3:17

Isn't it wonderful how we live in this microwave era, where everything is served quick, fast and in a hurry. You want popcorn? No problem. Put it in the microwave and just press popcorn. You don't even have to press how many minutes. You want breakfast? No problem, go in the freezer and get yourself a bacon and eggs, and a frozen biscuit, pop it in the microwave and wa-la, it's piping hot and ready to eat.

How about you just got off work, or school and your feet are hurting, kids are hollering for your attention, its evening time and you just want something to eat now? Either you cook from scratch, or you buy the famous store sale, ten for $10 wonderful microwave dinners. From meatloaf dinners, to spaghetti dinner, fried chicken, Salisbury steak, you name it. We are sisters and mommas trying to make it through another day with quick fixes. But first, before you shop, you just gotta stop by the delicatessen counter for a quick sample of today's wonderful, delicious, mouth watering, hot, cold, spicy, sweet, treats to help you through the aisles to spend your last dime until the next time. It's the in-the-meantime, meeting place to get a quick fix to curb that hunger pain, before you get home. You quickly pull your number as your eyes carefully measure the length and breath of the glass window where you can see, the fancy jello dishes and the wonderful fruit salads, and check out the savory salads, of sorts.

You're waiting patiently for your number to be called. You have decided now what you are going to try. Maybe a little chicken salad with the apples and walnuts, or maybe the seafood salad, and then you need a little dessert. You think, "I'll try the cream cheese cake, and then the chocolate mousse," and then the store clerk hollers number 84. "Yes!" you answer. You're hungry and you just can't say NO! It's FREE and you don't need to use manners. She gives you a cute little cup and spoon, and your eyes buy every sample you can try. May I have a little of this, and a little of that? As you walk away enjoying your sample, you're here, there and everywhere.

Before you know it, you're no longer hungry for your appetite has been pacified. In fact, you don't even want another sample, let alone buy what you just sampled. Yes, I know you have been there and done that.

Many times we say, "Yuck! That stuff was spoiled or down right nasty!

I'm glad I didn't buy that before I tried it. I'm glad they give out samples, so I didn't have to spend my money, or waste my time." You take your little cup and spoon, and search for a garbage can, so you can quickly discard the evidence.

Those little cups and spoons that you welcomed so hastily and with such desired anticipation now becomes an eye sore, and is quit frankly getting on your nerves to have around. You certainly didn't anticipate taking that trash home. It will be lucky if it makes it to the car. And, if by chance it makes it home, it was a mistake, and will soon find it's home on the curb on garbage pick up day.

How soon we forget the purpose of a sample! The ultimate purpose and reason of a free sample is to whet and pacify the appetite of the recipient, and hopefully it will sell itself. Sometimes it works, but most times, the sample never makes it to the dinner table for the family and friends to enjoy.

This chapter is sending out an S.O.S. to help out all our Christian sisters who have been laying down more than standing up in their Christian walk. We pray that all our Christian sisters take heed lest ye also fall.

[Warning: *this section may hurt your feelings, but surely will bless your soul!*]

Are you a Sample or a Saint?

First let me define the term Sample in this book. A sample is defined as a sinning saint. They spend more time in sin than they do in the sanctuary and they probably work more than they worship. A sample does not refer to a sinner [*non-Christian*], but an individual male or female who profess to be a Christian and is actively involved in sexual iniquity.

Yes it's true; men and women alike are filling their wicked appetites with the pleasures of sexual sampling, just as if they could just make a quick stop by a grocer store and get a free sample of sweet delights, and hot bites, to quickly pacify their sexual hunger just to find themselves emptied to indulge again and again.

To you our sisters who are giving out free samples—yes, I'm in the right book—our young Christian sisters are giving out sexual samples and for what? Our teen girls are engaging in sexual sins, at school, in the parking lot, at the park, at home when momma is working hard and you have been irresponsible to say the least.

I'm not going to fuss too much because maybe you have had some bad past experiences like maybe being raped or molested and no one knew. Maybe it was due to a date rape or some other unfortunate circumstance. Whatever the case may be, the fact, that you had no control over being hurt should give you more strength to STAND and take control over your choices now.

You're not alone, and maybe you are scared about the outcome of your new relationship, will it last. Since you were forced to be sexually active in the past you may feel that if you don't give it up, it will be taken again anyway. Don't speak that over your life. Think positive, be assertive about your wished to abstain from sexual sins, and let him know you are worth the wait. You will have the rest of your lives to enjoy making love.

We suggest that you get counseling if you have been hurt by rape or molested before you get married to help you sort out any unresolved issues you may have lingering in your heart concerning your abuse or abuser.

I just want to admonish you that you have a choice and this book is giving you options to help you make the right decisions, as you try to find your way through life hopefully with Christ as your guide.

Ecclesiastes 8:12 says "Though a sinner do evil an hundred times, and his days be prolonged, yet surely I know that it shall be well with them that fear God, which fear before him." God will bless you for fearing him enough to obey him, not because you don't love your spouse to be, but because you love God more; because he gave you your spouse to be; and you fear him enough to not mess that up. 1 Corinthians 5:1 reminds us that fornication is common in the church and such fornication as is not so much as named among the Gentiles, [*non-Christians*]. Even they aren't doing filthy, indecent, offensive, nasty stuff some sisters in the church are doing.

From a momma who has many daughters, I'm going to talk to you the same way I would speak to my daughters with just a little more grace for your soul sake. So if you don't have a church mother, I'm going to be your church mother in this book. I want to ask you a question: "What? know ye not that your body is the temple of the Holy Ghost which is in you, which ye have of God, and ye are not your own? For ye are bought with a price: therefore glorify God in your body, and in your spirit, which are God's" 1 Corinthians 6:19-20.

For a Christian woman, it's crucial that she keeps herself [*body, spirit, and soul*] until she is in a committed relationship because her body is her most precious asset. When she gives her body, her mind, heart, and strength go with it. So, when she makes love [*not sex*], she's giving with her body, her soul and spirit, and vice versa. If the woman has sex outside of the sanctity of marriage [*give a sample*] the man walks away, and takes a piece of her spirit with him in which she can never retrieve. Her good thing is now just another sample consumed in a moment of sexual hunger.

Proverb 30:18-19: "There be three things which are too wonderful for me, yea, four which I know not… …the way of a man with a maid."

In our Christian courtship, yes, we put forth our best effort to show our love and affection toward our soon to be spouse. In many ways just a little too much when some of you are pressured to do things that are not Christian-like at all. Let's face it, women are natural pleasers, and the men folk are squeezers. Men will squeeze you to please them, and if you allow yourself to be cornered in unsafe places you may become very sorry. It doesn't matter if you are grown.

Man is always seeking and searching out that which will please and satisfy his flesh. You, as a Christian woman, don't owe your flesh anything, and you certainly don't owe him [*his flesh*] anything. Romans 8:12 "Therefore, brethren, we are debtors, not to the flesh, to live after the flesh." God created sexual pleasure for the flesh of man in the sanctity of marriage. Yes, sometimes women feel the pressure of taking care of their man by helping him out in a sexual way. Let me share something with you. You don't have any business helping him out [*in any sexual way*] until he loves you enough to make you his wife. If he wants a sample let him go to the corner and pay for it, because yours ain't free or for sale.

Christians are examples not samples. You have many virtuous sisters for an ensample, so let us walk by the same rule, let us mind the same thing. Sisters be careful for nothing. [Take note, Philippians 4:6]. The worldly samples are voluptuous women who do, and the true example are the virtuous woman who chose not to.

We have a host of Christian heroes of faith. They followed God's Plan, and not Man's Plan. God's plan is for every man to have his own wife, and every woman to have her own husband.

Man's plan is like the woman in the Bible who had five husbands and the one she had wasn't hers [John 4:17-18]. Yes! You can be an example right now. God knows what you need, and his Word said he will supply your needs according to his riches in glory. If God should run out, can he not create it?

When God sends his best, his man will not be looking for the devil's mess. He may even bring you a test, and if you fail it he will have no problem changing his mind. So many sisters have given up a sample, and the morning after, their fiancé changed his mind. You will never know how many Christian sisters who have been cheated out of a wonderful married life, all because they fell for sometimes, a ninety-nine cent burger and a sack of fries.

He will say he needs more time, and leave you standing again in the single line. Sometimes, a godly man that is looking for a wife will test you to see if you are a sample or a saint. Why, because he is looking for the whole cake, a wife. If he can get a sample, from a woman who doesn't know her worth, it will always put a question mark in his mind, who else or how many others have gotten a sample from you before or after him. He may be spirit-filled, but he still thinks like a man and act like a man because he is a man. So, don't be so spiritual, that you think the only thing on his mind is the Holy scripture. He is looking for a wife, not a woman who is not wife material. He is looking for his good thing. Every man knows what a good thing is, that's what he will always look for when he wants to get married. He needs to know that he can trust you even before you say, "Yes, I will marry you." If he can't trust you before the marriage, how can he be sure he can trust you after the marriage when things get rough?

Don't be a learner of experience, but be a learner from an example. If you are involved in premarital sexual relations and you want to help a brother out? Go on a you-and-him-ain't-getting-none [*sex*] fast, and see how God will bless. If you are a virgin, I like to use this example to paint a picture of a virgin. She's like a Hershey Kiss, sweet and wrapped tight. Have you ever tried to rewrap a Hershey Kiss? Once unwrapped, the pleasure is sweet and short lived, you have to eat another and another and another to always get that first experience of the sweet joy a Hershey Kiss bring.

One is hardly ever enough. This is what happens to our sweet and innocent virgin sisters who don't know or understand who they are, and what God has created in us. We are a good "sweet" thing, and I can't say it enough. Every man who loves the woman that God has created will testify that we are good and very good. This is why men are always searching for that innocent virgin, because she is sweet and *Umm Umm good.*

He wants that experience again and again. Nevertheless, a mature Christian man wants a wife because he knows and understand that whether she is a virgin or not, due to divorce or other circumstances, if she is a spiritual Christian woman and loves the Lord, she will be a good "sweet" thing for him over and over again. And, because she has the sweet spirit of Christ in her, she will do him good and no harm all the days of her life.

Yes, it is comforting to have an example or pattern to follow in this Christian walk. Don't give away a free sample, to later sing the gospel blues about, if I were in control of my life I think that I would have worked things out differently. This is the time to do things differently, so you won't be singing the blues afterward.

I was having a conversation with a sister about why there are not many weddings in the church today. I was thinking, maybe it's because too many Christian sisters are giving out free samples. Why should a brother bother with courtship, the wedding planning, and all the wonderful things associated with being in love and getting married, when you can get a free sample? In fact, he's just a sampler. He's not serious about you or God.

God has not changed his moral standards to suit a profligate generation. Know ye not that the unrighteous shall not inherit the kingdom of God? Be not deceived: neither fornicators…shall inherit the kingdom of God. Let me remind you my Christian sister, the Bible says and such were some of you; but ye are washed, but ye are sanctified, [*separate/saints*] but ye are justified in the name of the Lord Jesus, and by the Spirit of our God. Whatever happened to the song you use to sing: "Things I use to do I don't do no more, and there's been a great change in me, since Jesus came into my life"? This is what you use to do – have sex before you became a Christian – so what happened?

Some of you Christian sisters, who are reading this book, are involved in sexual sins, you went from the first time you had sex, you were so condemned and ashamed, told God you would never do it again, to now using and practicing birth control methods. And some of you have gone as far as shedding innocent blood. Yes, having an abortion, and packing Plan B [*the morning after pill*] in your purse.

Somebody said sin will take you further than you wanted to go; cost you more that you intended to pay, and keep you longer than you intended to stay. Nevertheless, God loves you still but he hates the sin. Let me ask you a question: Have you even tried to stop having sex, or do you think that it's just what you do because you are engaged to marry? Even the world knows that sex outside of marriage is wrong, unsafe, and unadvisable. You can find abstinence classes in almost every school from the east coast to the west coast and all over our globe.

Teen peer pressure is hard, and you can't even imagine how hard it is for grown folks [*sisters*] who know what to do and how to do it. Nevertheless, it still stands true, if a man really cares about you, and loves you, he won't ask you to do something you don't want to do especially if he is also a true Christian. Unless, he is also non-Christian or a sinning saint. If he persistently pressures you to help him out, then I would suspect that you are probably in a relationship that is not of God. This is called unequally yoked to an unbeliever. He is a non-Christian.

Did you know that Christian sisters are those that practice abstinence not because it's a choice or option, but because it's a way of life for all single Christians? Hebrews 13:4, "Marriage is honorable in all, and the bed undefiled: but whoremongers and adulterers God will judge." My sister, wait on God and don't cheat yourself out of a wonderful blessing. Don't miss out on ever knowing how good it truly is to wait. You ask, "What do I do if I want to stop?"

Good question. First, tell Jesus. 1 John 1:9 promises, if we confess our sins, God is faithful and just to forgive us our sins, and to cleanse us from all unrighteousness. Next seek council. Proverb 24:6 instructs, for by wise counsel thou shalt make thy war: and in multitude of counselors there is safety. Brush the dust off your Bible and start reading it because if you have been commonly indulging in sexual activities you need the word of God to cleanse your heart. Read, practice, and memorize, and go and sin no more.

Psalm 51:1-2, 17

"[1]Have mercy upon me, O God, according to thy lovingkindness:
according unto the multitude of thy tender mercies
blot out my transgressions. [2]Wash me throughly from mine iniquity,
and cleanse me from my sin."
"[17]The sacrifices of God are a broken spirit; a broken and a contrite heart,
O God, thou wilt not despise."

The problems we have in the church today is we have more sisters who are samples instead of saints, and it's not God's fault.

RULE 10:

Mood Music 101

"Speaking to yourselves in psalms and hymns and spiritual songs,
singing and making melody in your heart to Yahuah [יהוה];
Giving thanks always for all things unto God and the Father
in the name of our Lord Jesus [יהושע Yahushua] the Christ."
Ephesians 5:19-20

Being a preacher's daughter, I was in church seemingly as much as in school. During many Bible Study classes, the subject matter would often come up about mood music for courting Christian couples. Questions like what's appropriate for Christian lovers? Or what's wrong with jazz or non-Christian instrumentals? Personally at the time, I couldn't relate because I was already married. I thought it was obvious that whatever music you listened to as a Christian before you entered into your courtship, you still listened to the same music.

I wasn't interested in that subject, so I thought, "Pastor please get on with the Bible Class." I had no clue that couples were changing the radio station because they were in a courtship. Somehow Christian couples felt like they needed some atmosphere help to put them in the mood of love.

Wow! If you need some mood music, maybe you're not in love. Let me tell you, if you are truly in love, love don't need and never will need mood music. Love makes its own music and plays its own song. The aura of love itself is so fulfilling, it doesn't need some music to help you keep your mind high and lifted up – *That's if you are really in love.*

Absolutely, it is better to marry than to burn. Let me ask you this, if a fire was already burning, would you say, "Something is wrong with that fire; let me add another log and strike another match." Common sense would not allow you to strike a match on fire that's already burning! Then who's going to put the fire out? This is what mood music does when you put it on. It is symbolic to adding another log on a pile of logs that is already burning. It is a fire that is well lit, hot and ready to roast whatever is in its path. This is why the Apostle Paul said it is better to marry than to burn. When you are in love you are burning, or soon will be, point blank. However, for the intellectual, here's to your "mood" music 101.

    Let me first define the word mood; and then I'm going to give you a biblical view on music to help our more intellectual sisters [*those of you who need verse and scripture*]. Mood: a state of mind in which an emotion or set of emotions gains ascendancy [*domination*]. Mood: temper, affection, character, disposition, personality, response, feeling, emotion, etc., These are the areas that will be affected by something that will enter your ear gate, and your mood, it will take domination [*control*] and put you in an emotional state of mind that can and will cause you to do good or evil.

    Let's see. What mood do you want to be in when you are with your soon to be husband? Here are a few choices; you chose. So let's imagine for a moment that you are with your sweetheart and you want to listen to some "mood" music, so you go to your cable [MC] music choice alternatives cable channel, iPod, Blackberry, Internet, or radio station which plays mood music for everyone, and music for every mood. Look at the different choices of mood music listed and pick the mood you want to be in. Go ahead; you've got time. Circle your FM dial below.

    We'll call these the Mood Music 101 FM [*your Favorite Music*] Stations.

- **101.1 FM** – Turn up the bass as international DJ's hit you with phat beats, pulsating sounds and exclusive hour-long mixes you can't hear anywhere else.
- **101.2 FM** – Keep it moving with the biggest club mixes and the hottest international DJ compilations 24/7 Dance til you drop.
- **101.3 FM** – Urban adult music from yesterday and today, plus sultry slow jams for the grown and sexy. R&B Soul, R&B Hits etc.,

101.4 FM – Swing on through the doors of the opry and step back in time to your kind of country. Classis Country, Blue Grass, Hip-Hop etc.

101.5 FM – Get the party started with a mix of good-time tracks from the 60s to the present. Party favorites, 80s, and 90s etc.

101.6 FM – A mix of slow and mid-tempo plays hits from lite hits, adults top 40 etc.,

101.7 FM – Experience the new rock revelation on music choice rock, and classic

101.8 FM – Slip into a pair of bellbottoms and trip back to when love was free, peace was the sign of the times and polyester was the fiber of choice. 70s, solid gold oldies, smooth jazz or just jazz.

101.9 FM – Jump and jive to the rich sounds of an era when bandleaders were kings of swing. Big Bang and Swing singers and standards…

102.1 FM – Get your mojo working with everything from electrifying Chicago sounds to Mississippi Delta Blues. Reggae, easy listening etc.,

102.2 FM – Wrap yourself with the warm feelings of remembrance of string orchestras and great instrumentals. Blues, Reggae, Soundscapes, Easy listening

102.3 FM – Sounds of the season enjoy the holidays with tunes that capture the spirit of the season.

102.4 FM – Catch breakneck picking and high-tonesome singing straight off the mountain from the masters. Blue Grass, etc.,

102.5 FM – Lift your spirit with the best of traditional and contemporary gospel music.

What did you choose? Keep it there and let's see if it was a wise choice when you are finished reading this rule.

If you allow yourself to be placed in a peculiar situation, surrounded by an ungodly atmosphere of worldly [*mood*] music, you are at a dangerously high risk to become another one to bite the dust, and succumb to an evil end that was supposed to be a sweet and innocent end. If you chose the wrong mood music, you are on the devil's territory.

1 Peter 4:1-2 "For as much then as Christ hath suffered for us in the flesh, arm yourselves likewise with the same mind: for he that hath suffered in the flesh hath ceased from sin; that he no longer should live the rest of his time in the flesh to the lust of men, but to the will of God.

His music will take you further than you wanted to go, it will keep you longer than you wanted to stay, and cost you more than you intended to pay. Sin begins in the mind, and if he [*the devil*] can get his music in your mind, he's won half the battle in devising your fall. It's like driving a Mack Truck with a blindfold on. It is almost certain that you will not make it to the altar pure and undefiled, if you don't hurry up and find the right mood music to help you keep your mind on God and not on your flesh.

So, in that vein, stay clear of house calls, yours or his. You're courting so do it in public places that are non-threatening to your soul, your spirit, and your body. Don't ever trust yourself or let me say don't ever trust your flesh. It is not saved, neither can it be. You are in a courtship. He's courting you, so let him do so. Spend quality time together at the park, museums, and with family and friends, etc.

Let him show you the world. Don't allow your courting days to be filled with complacency and the fulfillments of his needs. You are both in a courtship. Everything you think you want to do, do it. Reach for the sky, shoot at the moon. Someone said if you aim high enough you are bound to reach something. Time is a terrible thing to waste. Don't put yourself in a position to have a lot of time on your hands doing nothing. Did you know that sitting idle, places you in the position to feel like you need some help to fill the atmosphere, trying to pass the time away with "mood" music?

This is where mood music becomes the subject matter, when YOU, my sister, should be the subject matter, quite frankly. Music affects you mind, body, soul and spirit. Out of the five senses that God has given us, the two that influence our minds and hearts the most are the eyes and the ears. As Christian women in Courtship we are to guard our purity at all cost, and not allow anything that is not pleasing in the eyes and ears of our heavenly Father to enter our eyes and ear gate. Through our ears we hear its sounds.

The information we receive makes a direct impression upon our thinking and our feelings which affect our mood. Read this again!

Music expresses the thoughts and emotions of an author, which, in turn, are shared with his audience. Therefore, music is a form of religious fellowship. It is religious because thoughts and emotions are always moral, and it is fellowship because of the sharing between author and audience.

For the Christian this imposes a serious responsibility. We are entreated by the spirit of Christ to avoid music that promotes thoughts and emotions contrary to the Word of God. We are to enjoy music that lifts the spirits of its listeners. Art and music are exclusively the creations of God and not man. Because art and music express thoughts and emotions, they exert a moral influence on our behavior. For this reason, we need to use them in harmony with God's word. Music is composed of three basic elements: melody, harmony, and rhythm.

Let's see how the three relates to us and mood music. Melody corresponds to the mind because it consists of a series of related tones that express a music idea. Harmony corresponds to the emotions. It relates the mood and colors the state of mind expressed in the melody. Harmony consists primarily of major and minor chords. Major chords more positive, give a feeling of certainty, happiness, or joy, minor chords are more negative and gives a feeling of uncertainty, sadness, or even depression.

These are the primary structure. Rhythm corresponds to the senses. For example, when people dance, they do not dance to the melody or the harmony, but to the rhythm. Finally, the tempo determines how fast or how slow, which can affect a person's pulse rate and adrenaline. [*The slower the music, the more under its influence you are. As an example, think of how the closer a person is to death, the slower the heart beat*]. You can put ungodly mood music, drugs, and alcohol, in the same category; they all dull the senses and cause you to not be in your right mind and will cause you to have a crazy mood. Satan comes to kill, steal, and destroy your virtuous reputation if he has to altar your mood through music to do so.

Ungodly music is any music that doesn't bring glory and honor to our Heavenly Father. The power and influence of music can and are used for both good and evil. As Christians we should not allow the tempter the devil to deceive you in thinking that it's only a love song for lovers. God has love songs for his children to sing and enjoy, and the devil has love songs for his children to sing and enjoy.

Let me add this note. What we see and hear are to always be in harmony with God's truth and morality. My sister, the devil wants to sift you as wheat; this book is here to help you keep your purity intact for a testimony of excellence. He [*the devil*] understands the power and influence music has on the body, spirit, and soul of man. He was created an instrument of praise, the master musician. He was created to bring pleasure and honor to God through music. Likewise, the devil's music is use to bring pleasure, glory and honor to its creator.

Now his musical talents and abilities only bring displeasure and dishonor to God. When you chose his [the devil's] music, your actions, your thoughts, your attitude, your ways, your spirit, and you bring displeasure and dishonor to God. Music provokes good and evil. Remember when King Saul summoned David to play the evil spirits off him.

THINK! If good music played [**by an anointed godly musician**] can get evil spirits off a man, then why is it so hard to believe that evil music played [**by an ungodly musician**] can put bad and evil influence on a good man?

You didn't need him [*the devil*] or his music to fall in love, and you don't need him or his music to stay in love. Satan is the god of this world; his music has cause many virgins to lose their virginity because they were wooed by his [*ungodly*] mood music. God's music will never cause you to sin against him. Stay in the right mood, and let your conversation be holy. Let your lover be reminded that he is standing on holy ground, and there are angels standing all around, to keep you from falling. Worldly [*ungodly*] mood music will put you to spiritual death, one lyric at a time, if you don't allow the word of God to help keep you rooted and grounded. It's a set up and don't fall for it.

Now let's go back to your mood music of choice. What did you set your dial on? If you are a Christian that means that you have Christ inside of you. If he is inside of you, then there should not be anything outside of you that you associate yourself with that will offend him, from ungodly friends to ungodly music.

If it would offend God, it should offend you. Remember Lot [2 Peter 2:8] in the wicked days of Sodom and Gomorrah, it says for that righteous man dwelling among them, in seeing and hearing, vexed his righteous soul from day to day. If Christ were to walk in the room with the mood music you love to hear, would you change the station or keep it there?

God used the anointed music of David to play the distressed spirit out of Saul; [1 Samuel 16:16-23] we'll say it again. If anointed music can play the devil out and usher the spirit of God in, then demonic music can play sin in and usher the spirit of God out. Your godly spirit ought not want to be a partaker or around anyone who doesn't want to be around your God, your pastor, God's people, God's music, and anything that is Godly. If they say it don't take all that, whatever you have in your hands drop it and run as fast and as far away from that person as you can get. Don't leave an address, a phone number, your email address, your friend's number, momma's number, sister, brother or anyone who can help that person get in touch with you ever!

RULE 11:

Courtship With Children

Momma, Her Children and Her Man

This is a special chapter for all mothers in courtship with children. As a mother who has birthed nine natural children into this world, grandmother, and stepmother, I would do you an injustice by not including this important topic of courting with children.

My first marriage started as a pregnant teen in the twelfth grade. I was a pastor's daughter, who through disobedience brought shame and disgrace upon the family's good name by getting pregnant out of wedlock. Everything a pastor preaches against, I became victim. I tried to do the right thing for the wrong reason. We went to City Hall after school one day and eloped. I got up the next day and went to school. No courtship, no honeymoon, no prom, and no bridal shower. The only present I received when I got married was an alarm clock from my mom. She was so afraid I wouldn't graduate. I went from Momma's house to his house and stayed twenty-five plus years, and nine kids later. Yes! I can say been there, done that, wore the t-shirt, and now wrote the book. I still say, two wrongs don't ever make things right. Never try to make things right for the wrong reasons. Years into my first marriage I was always trying to do the right thing for the wrong reason. At the top of the list was pleasing people. I began seeking God for inner peace for my spirit and soul. Nothing would satisfy. Eight years into my marriage at the tender age of twenty-six years old, God filled my soul with His Holy Spirit. I stayed married for another eighteen years.

From that wonderful day that God filled my soul with the Holy Ghost,

I was able to stay saved and sane with all my pain, until God said, "Enough is Enough." After my divorce, I began my new Christian life as a single mother with nine children. I now had the dual role of parenting and all the unforeseen difficulties that millions of single mom's face all over this world. That's another book.

In spite of all the adverse conditions and dysfunctional family problems I was facing, all I wanted was to do those things that were right and pleasing in the eyes of God. I was happy in Jesus. I was out of Egypt and enjoying Canaan land, flowing with endless possibilities of the things I could freely do for my God and Savior as an unmarried woman.

I kept busy taking care of my children, loving my "me" time and determined to get off welfare. I went back to college and completed my Real Estate credit hours to return back into the field of being a Realtor. I took great pleasure in doing Kingdom business and taking care of my children, bringing them up in the fear and admonition of the Lord. I loved it, but I was one broke, happy sister. My needs were met, and I lived within my means.

I was at home one evening just minding my own business when I received a phone call from a pulchritudinous [*sanctified*] Prince. He said to me, "I'm not looking for a girlfriend. I'm looking for a wife. God told me it was you. If you need to pray about it, I will give you all the time you need. I'm not going anywhere until you give me an answer. I'll have to fill you in with a few other details later." I must tell you a whole lot was said and happened between this paragraph and the one before it, so I'll start here with the courtship of Momma [*myself*], my children and her man, the Prince.

There I was, over forty-five years old—they say over the hill momma—at home with nine children [*two of which were my grandchildren*]. I was a welfare mom, renting a home because I lost my house in the divorce, and other unimportant issues to wit, and I am favored with an invitation to marry. After I answered, "Yes, I will marry you!" the courtship was on. I never ate out so much in my entire life. From breakfast, lunches, candlelight dinners, flowers, and candy, there was a whirlwind of love and affection shown towards me every minute of the day. I never talked on the phone so much in all my adult life. Often times I talked so much my phone would be literally hot; I would have to hang up so the phone would cool itself off.

We talked morning, noon and night. There was hardly a day, that we didn't see one another. As soon as I was able to let go and allow myself to love, I began falling deeply in love. At first I was in love with the thought of being in love. Later I allowed myself to be in love and to be loved. God really blessed me to have someone in my life that was so easy to love, I could hardly look into his eyes because I wanted to keep my thoughts pure. I mean after all I was married before, so I understood the joy of sex marriage offered. Yes! Sanctified folks are the most passionate loving people on this earth. If you haven't met one keep looking. Read the *Book of Solomon*, he is the most passionate and romantic preacher in the Bible. If anybody should know how to love, it should be God's people!

Nevertheless, neither one of us had any courtship experience as Christians before. Our first marriages were very similar, jumped in young, inexperienced and without God. Now we have entered into our new courtship for the first time starting out with God in our lives. We were beginning a new courtship with Jesus as our chaperone, teaching us how to have a godly courtship and keeping it holy. It's like being handed a new born baby with no instructions. You learn as you go. However, this is why I wrote this book. You're in love, and your head is truly in the clouds. You need some help!

I was in love with this man and in love with being in love. I felt like a virgin all over again, and he was about to be my first love. He poured it on and made me feel truly loved. He swept me off my feet; my head was—no doubt about it—on cloud nine. I went from holding children's hands to holding a man's hand. Let me tell you, it's not an easy task, especially, when you are used to leading and not following. I had to laugh at myself when we would be walking together and sometimes I would find it hard to coordinate my steps with his. Yes, that's right; coordinate your steps with his. When you are use to walking alone, you don't give it a second thought about being in sync, walking in harmony step by step with anyone. [*That's a message within itself*]. I was use to walking alone, driving alone, going to church alone, going to the schools on parent-teachers night alone, going to the store alone, sleeping alone, eating alone, being alone, without a man, boyfriend, etc. So yes, I was so clumsy. I just downright felt embarrassed.

Really, there was no need for me to feel embarrassed because we were in a courtship and its part of the process, coming together as one. Learning how to walk and talk together physically, naturally and spiritually. So don't feel embarrass about any clumsiness you may experience, just have a few laughs. It's good for the soul and the relationship.

We had practically everything in common. We went to the same church, were both in the ministry, loved and worshipped the same God. We loved the same foods, had many of the same dreams, and desires. We wanted the same things in life, and we were head over heels in love with each other. We were truly compatible in so many ways it was alarming and delightful. It was more than I ever expected. You'll find out that when you get older your expectations and demand list narrows down to realities and necessities. Give us that and we're happy, if we get more we are ecstatic. I was ecstatic. If I ever decide to write a *Cloud Rules II* book, I will tell you some wonderful things because they are too much for this book. He's my Sunshine and I his Rainbow. As my grandson described to us one of the things we had in common, he said, "You have the same eyes." Wow! He saw love in our eyes at the age of six years old.

I have experienced a true life Cinderella story, an encouragement to you. Cinderella always get her man. When the Prince came to her door with the glass slipper she was at home minding her own business, and her midnight turned into day. All odds according to statistics would say that a single, divorced welfare mom over forty-five with nine children getting married is one in a million. But when you take care of God's business he will take care of yours, and you will be that one in a million. Jeremiah 10:23 says, "O Yahuah [יהוה], I know that the way of man is not in himself: it is not in man that walketh to direct his steps." And Jeremiah continues 17:7 "Blessed is the man that trusteth in Yahuah [יהוה], and whose hope the Lord is."

Going into my first marriage at eighteen, I didn't know what to do with myself, or what life steps to take that would bring me blessings or cursing without acknowledging God. When I became a mature woman, I learned to trust God. I had never experienced such love in my life like this before; and now, I had nine carts before the horse. What do you do with the kids when you are in love and find yourself in a Christian courtship?

I didn't have a clue or a book to read to help me with some very common issues I had with courting with children and therefore, I learned some very hard and valuable lessons that if I could do some things over again, I certainly would have. My word of experience to you is, be a learner of an example and not from experience. It can be devastating and costly. Old folks call it bought sense.

Courting with children for me was more difficult than having nine children. The first two and a half years of my new marriage were the best years of my life and the worst years of parenting. They were the best years as far as being in love and being loved in returned. This chapter of my life was a prove-me chapter. If my husband truly didn't have the spirit of God in his life and really married me because he loved me, I don't believe my new marriage would have survived the turbulences and aftermath of my first marriage post divorce issues, even though I had already been divorced several years before my courtship even started.

I'm convinced that had I continued to be a struggling welfare mom raising nine children, I would not have written this book. But God, by his grace kept us, and his love fortified us. God was preparing me and making me ready for the spiritual warfare I was about to face. I felt the worst part was fighting with the court system and my children's father to relocate our kids to my new home out of state. I thought I could just pack up and move with my new husband and live happily ever after. WRONG!

New rule – if you remarry it is very possible and even the law [*check your state laws*] that if you are going to relocate to another state the noncustodial parent has the legal right to stop you from successfully removing your children from the state. This law is effective if you were married in the same state and live in the same state or neighboring state. This is true for Illinois. If you married in Illinois and both parents live in Illinois after the divorce, the noncustodial parent can take you back to court if you try to remove and relocate minor children. You can win, as I did but prepare for war. It can be a devastating and costly battle.

I traveled over 12,000 miles in one year to fight for our kids summer, spring, winter and fall. Many times I felt like giving up and letting the kids be raised by their father. I traveled through rain storms, snow storms, ice storms, and even a blow-out on the highway hundreds of miles from home with two children and no road side service. [*sisters don't neglect your road side service, which I thought I had at the time*]. I fought against sleep deficit, weariness and just being plain tired and drained, many times spiritually, mentally, physically, emotionally, and financially. Talking about the devil wearing out the saints! He was on my heels, breathing threats of discouragements and frustrations. I just had to hold on. Oh, the stories I could tell. Many times I was angry and fearful, but it wasn't over yet.

Often times God would remind me that every time I fought for my kids, he had a blessing waiting for me when I returned home. Absence really does make the heart grow fonder. My new husband was always supportive of me. He had my back. Here I was a newlywed, and before my feet could touch the ground from the high altitude of the clouds I was in court. I was in court so much I had to home school three of my kids to keep up with my court appearances. Let me testify, it was costly but God had that too. The end result was that my kids were all placed in their rightful grade the following school year, not missing a beat. My other three children who lived with their father in another state also passed to the next school year not missing a beat. It was a horrible parenting year for me. I never thought I would be a long-distance parent, advising and chastising via telephone visits. When I reflect back, I truly wish I had enjoyed the time I had with the three kids I had with me. I was so busy being upset about not having all six kids with me; but God was giving me and my new husband a break our first years of marriage. We truly don't understand when God is just trying to give us a break.

    I do regret not blessing God as I really should have; because I was so busy fighting the air when God knew I was going to win all the time. As a mom I felt the separation from the other three kids to be unbearable because I always assumed that they would always be with me. Here's another tip, don't take your kids for granted. They can be with you today, and somewhere else tomorrow. It was like tearing three kids out of my arms, and I couldn't do anything about it. Had I known that it was going to turn out fine, I would have done things differently like got my hair and nails done more often, instead of worrying about the next financial burden of my court appearance. All my kids are together now so everything worked out great. Now one thing I must say to the men folk that might read this chapter. Hurray for my children's father. I must agree, as much as it hurt to have gone through such an ordeal, I have to respect the fact that he fought a good fight. But God was in charge and in control.

    Let me help a sister that may have similar issues. If your child[ren]'s father fight for his children [*reasons are irrelevant*], don't ever give up your children because you are tired of the battle. Remember, it's not about you when you are a Christian, it's about God. God has given you a mandate to train up your child in the fear and admonition of our Heavenly Father.

    When God knows he can trust us to rear our children in the way of truth and righteousness, you will win. During the meantime struggle, never give up your parental rights. Always stay in your kids face, even via phone. Talk with their teachers and the school principal. Go to the school and pick up their grade reports. It will be alright. Trust God. He just wants to know how bad do you want to raise your child to love and honor him. He will not put more on you than you can handle. Do you want it bad enough to fight until you no longer have a fight in you? The Bible admonishes us that "If you faint in the day of adversity, your strength is small" Proverb 24:10. When you need strength, ask God for more strength. Many times I had to just praise and pray my way through. I said to someone, "I'm just going through." They said to me, "Well go on through then!" So you say, you're going through –then go on through, don't stop, after you have done all you can do, stand and God will give you the victory. The fervent prayers of the righteous man does avail much [James 5:16]. Every parent good or bad has a legal right to fight for his or her children, but God has the last say. I'm going to tell you like the song, I couldn't give up; I had come too far from where I started from.

I didn't have my mom to tell me it was going to be all right. I just had to believe with God on my side it was going to be all right. You, too, just can't give up now. You've come too far from where you have started. God has placed this book in your hands, because he cares deeply for you. You are engraved in the palms of his hands [Isaiah 49:16]. Don't you believe the lie that you won't make it. You not only will make it, but you will have a testimony that won't ever spoil.

First and foremost, stay focused. Children are the heritage of the Lord; they don't belong to us, but God. God has seen fit to make us stewards over them. If you should find yourself in such a dilemma don't stress. First, bless God and know that you're gonna win in the end. Second, don't be anxious for anything. It may not be as bad as it seems. Prepare for spiritual battle. Don't take insults personally. The devil is just mad that God is so blessing you. Don't embarrass God. Remember God's word, "be not overcome with evil, but overcome evil with good" [Romans 12:21]. No matter how long it takes, no weapon formed against you shall prosper. He that shall come, will come, and will not tarry. When it's over, it's over. The devil can't add another weight on the balance.

As a single parent, I know you may be very excited about the prospects of right-now help from a soon to be spouse. As soon as you marry you may be thinking that the stepparent will immediately assume the non-custodial parent role. If he does, that's great; if he doesn't don't get bent out of shape. Please don't put that kind of confidence in any man, or that kind of pressure on the stepparent and the children. Remember when your head is in the clouds, his will be too, even if they don't admit it.

After the marriage [*and honeymoon if you are able to have both*] and you begin to keep house and combined families, everything will or should be new to everyone. That's if you have not lived together previously. The kids have to get to know him as a live-in parent and the stepparent has to get to know the kids in the same manner as well.

For the sake of your children, we pray that you and your new companion are in complete harmony with God, for the continuance of their Christian upbringing in the fear, and admonition of the Lord. This is why it is so important for you to not be unequally yoked. You should start out on the same page in Christian values, morals, and goals.

Some women have built a very close and loyal relationship with their children. Their children have become their companion, and friend. Depending on how long you have been a single parent, some women are so close to their children that they won't make a move or major decision without consulting them. Take note, when you get married, understand that your children will not have the last say, or will even be involved in many adult decisions concerning family matters. If you are that sister, I employ you to consider weaning your children from this child/adult role that will become a problem for you in the marriage. Don't allow this to become a problem in your new marriage, that is if you intend to stay married. God commanded that a man leave his father and mother, and cleave to his wife; they shall be one flesh. What, therefore, God hath joined together, let not man put asunder. This means everyone, including your children. Help your child stay a child as long as you can.

Remember, you are the one in love with your husband, not your children. You love him; they hopefully will come to love him. It is his responsibility to love them and be so kind to them that they can't help but to love him. They will love him as a person. If they love him as a person then it's automatic that they will love him as their stepparent. Pray that you marry a kind and loving man, not just kind and loving to you, but also to your children. As a sister who has experienced this, here are a few things I would like to share with you.

After your pastor has been notified and has given his blessings [*hopefully*], your children should be the first of all family members to be notified of your engagement and intent to marry. Everyone else can come in any order you chose. Whether, best girlfriend, your parent, the non-custodial parent, etc., depending on the order and relationship you have with those that matter to you most. The reason you should tell your children first [*alone, then with your fiancé*] is because they are the ones that will be living with the person that you will commit to spending your life. They will have to accept and come to know your new love and companion who will be their stepfather. This will not be easy for some families. Some of you may have already shared your plans with your child or children about the possibilities of marrying even before the engagement. If you have done so already and this have worked for you that's good.

After you have officially talked with them, listen to their thoughts, and from that conversation on, never forget about their feelings. It doesn't mean you will like all the things that they will say or do. You will just know how to respond if you stay tuned to their feelings. It's their feelings about the new relationship or the new stepfather to be that will motivate them to act out positively or negatively during the entire process of the courtship and even into the marriage.

Some of the biggest problems you may possibly face could be your children's father, their affection, boundaries, and space when the new parent arrives as a new live-in member of the family. They will test you to know that you still love them as much as you did before.

Children are children and they are experts at playing the parent card. They know you better than most parents know their own children. Therefore, they will fight for your affection; competing to make you chose one or the other. They don't understand that you can have a win/win situation and not a win/lose situation. If you find yourself experiencing this, be patient. Escalating your emotions will not work in this case. Nevertheless, however long it takes, it will get worked out in time. Some family's timetable may be longer than others, especially if you still have court issues.

It will take time to work through the process of putting the proper things in place as God has destined. Allow God to help you lovingly and compassionately put the horse before the cart. And be not overcome with evil, but overcome evil with good. Whatever, you may be facing, remember, Romans 8:28, "And we know that all things work together for good to them that love God, to them who are the called according to his purpose." Don't let the devil push you to making God ashamed. Don't give your children up; fight for them, no matter what. You are the better choice, just by having Christ in your life makes the difference. Later in time, that difference will be ingrained into your children. They may act like they hate you now, but stand your ground, and let God fight your battle. He promised that no weapon formed against you shall prosper. Yes, you may lose a few battles, but God will make that devil pay you back double for your trouble.

Unfortunately, because of the dysfunction of divorces, children who are in the middle of their parents issues may feel responsible for either the separation or responsible for not getting their parents back together. They are idealist, and become very creative in their quest to make your courtship a battle of affection, and decisions. Pick your territory, your armor, and your weapon, because if you find yourself in this situation, it will be on. Start out with some wisdom and guidance. "Hear instruction, and be wise, and refuse it not" Proverb 8:33.

Your territory should begin with ground rules. First rule you want a win/win, not win/lose situation. Your armor should be you are the one in control and in charge. Your most powerful weapon of choice is love and prayer. Always, making every effort, assuring them that your love for them has not change, and that you will make adjustment so that everyone will have their time and space.

Don't take a sabbatical from being the loving parent; love whenever it is needed. Remember, Proverb 29:17, "Correct thy son, and he shall give thee rest; yea, he shall give delight unto thy soul." When we are in love, sometimes we become too lenient, because maybe we have temporarily stopped preparing a few home cooked meals and replaced dinner with burgers and fries, and they missed a few bed time stories, or whatever the case may be, thus allowing our children to play us. They get away with things that we would not ordinarily allow to get by on the sly. You must take the time to discipline or things will get out of hand. Make the time up in other ways but don't substitute discipline for lost time you can't get back.

Courting with Children Tips

New relationships take much cooperation and tolerance from everyone, momma, stepfather, and children. Blending families can be a very difficult and challenging process to say the least.

These rules will also apply whether or not you are a divorcee:
- if you are raising your grandchildren
- if the father is absent or not
- if you have not been married before
- if you are a foster parent or have children for whatever reason

I'm going to start by sharing with you some professional help tips I received when I was going through my dysfunctional ordeal called divorce.

First, have you ever heard about people taking other people's medicine? You know like an individual who has a medical problem, and can't afford to buy their medicine, so they call someone who they know have the same ailment, and take the same medicine, and borrow some until they can get their own. Yes, this is a fact, and it happens.

Well, I don't mind you borrowing some of my professional counseling medicine, as long as you get your own as soon as you can.

- Go to at least one [*or as many as needed*] premarital stepparent counseling session. In the state of Illinois, this is a pre-divorced requirement called **Focus on Children** for parents who are in the court system. This is the judicial system last attempt to see if the parents really want to go through with the divorce, and for the parents to understand the depths of how it will affect the children after the divorce. I personally feel [*having had my new husband attending with me*] that it should also be a stepparent requirement as well. Therefore, I highly recommend this. Even if you have never been married, this may prove to be something that will help your family in the long run.

- Allow your children to be a part of the courtship, so they can feel a part of the relationship. Yes, occasionally take them out to eat, play, and spend quality time with their soon-to-be stepfather. They, as well as you, need this experience. If they do embarrassing things, take care of it at the appropriate time. Don't behave like them. You are the adult; they are the children. Kids truly will be kids; they are what they are and do what they do.

• If you are able, and depending upon the relationship you have with the child's non-custodial parent, set up at least one official meeting for the non-custodial parent and the new stepparent to be introduced. If this is not possible, don't stress. One of the main reasons is because it makes the children feel significant. As I had to learn and understand that a child is 50% mom and 50% dad [*good or bad*]. To minimize further dysfunction, the custodial parent has the responsibility of building and protecting our children's self worth, their self esteem by acknowledging the other 50% of who they are, thereby acknowledging 100% of who they are. This does in no wise mean that you have to mimic the TV sitcom [*situation comedy*] shows One on One, or All of Us, etc., It's only a meeting to introduce the children's stepparent to be to the children's non-custodial parent. It can be at a park, fast food restaurant, or a place that you chose. The scheduled meeting time should be tolerable for all concerns. This is proper premarital protocol, whether or not you do it, is strictly your business.

• Discuss what will be the rules of engagements, concerning discipline, who's in charge, and where do we go from here [*new parental discipline rules after marriage*].

• Discuss being on the same page as parents, what will be acceptable and unacceptable.

• Discuss visitation of non-custodial parent, and child support issues, how would it affect the family income, without the support or children, if they change residence.

• Discuss the possibilities of sudden change, if custody of children were to change.

• Discuss what is expected if a child is about to be emancipated [*become the age of adulthood 18/21*]. Would they be expected to continue living with custodial parent? What about their health care issues, etc.

• Discuss the rules of engagement if grown children are living with custodial parent before marriage, and what is expected of them in regards to chores, or monetary obligations, or college after your new marriage.

• Discuss how long they are to be supported by custodial parent if they don't have any income, not in school or have a job after marriage. As it should be [*even though not always the case*] when married all income become household income, and not separate income. The other spouse husband or wife that has grown children living in the house with the new mate may not agree that your grown child continuing to be financially supported after a while. Do you have a plan? If not, get one!

• Discuss rearing live-in grandchildren: Are you expected to continue or do your spouse have other ideas that may be contrary to what you are now doing? A new spouse may want to go places, travel and do things. It may become a future problem if you say, "I can't go because I'm babysitting or raising my grandchild or grandchildren." You may want to discuss these things with your child and gradually make adjustments now or at least think about making plans to have someone to care for your grandchildren at a moment's notice if your new husband wants to take you away for a week-end or two week sabbatical. Something to think on especially if you are marrying into ministry. Remember God's word, let no man put asunder. If you are not ready for this, rethink whether you are ready for marriage.

• Tax purposes – If you are one of the rare parents who receive any form of child support, your child support may become in jeopardy in regards to your divorce decree or separation agreement. Ask questions concerning who can file the child[*ren*]. How will the child support be affected when you remarry? See a tax consultant, or go to a respectable source to help you sort out all possibilities, especially if the child[*ren*] will continue to live with you, or change residence to live with the non-custodial parent. How would you handle this change? Think on it for possibilities.

RULE 12:

Don't Be No Fool!

"A fool uttereth all his mind, but a wise man keepeth it in till afterwards. Proverb 29:11

This chapter wants to warn you about the dangers of talking too much. What you talk about now can hurt you or the old folks say come back to haunt you later. So, I will try to mention a few things that may relate to you now in your relationship that is a no-no, and a definite for goodness sake no, please sister, you wanna think before telling that.

This chapter is directed to those in absolutely new relationships. If your relationship is three to six months old, you probably have already done a lot of no-no's already. It's something how a man can say "I love you" and within three months he has the keys to your car, your apartment or home. He knows where you bank, have used your ATM card etc, and what else can I say. And you probably have done much of the same, from feeding his dog, putting his clothes in the cleaners, cleaned his last week dishes, made his bed, washed the ring out the tub… Stop, Stop, Stop, Lord, Stop!

Pray, "Lord please, help me not to be no fool." You are in a courtship that will go by so fast you will want to kick yourself for spending precious time, playing the wifie/the Mrs. before the I do's. To you my middle-aged sister, who now chooses cereal for the fiber and not the toy, you don't have time to be stuck on "capital S" stupid! Take this time and allow yourself to be wooed and not worked. God has blessed you just as he has blessed me to do it again and I would hate to hear you crying the sanctified blues, "If I had control of my life, I would have done things differently."

Well, you are in control NOW! You don't have to prove anything. Trust comes with time. He doesn't have to have every key to your lock[s] to prove you trust him. There is nothing more undignified than a mature sister to go completely silly. We mature sisters have a standard to uphold for our immature and inexperience sisters to emulate—don't drop the ball.

If you've just met him, you probably don't know him very well as of yet. Ok, girls, here we go. First of all, we hope that you are getting married because you are really in love with this person and want to spend the rest of your life in a monogamous marriage as husband and wife. You are looking forward to having a wonderful blessed and happy family and you're making plans to do so. The first thing you should have in common right now is great communications. You have been talking, more to him than anyone including your best friend, family and children if you have any. When you just think about him, the phone began to ring, and when you pick up the phone to call him, he's already on the line. Yes, it's an awesome feeling.

The older you are and the more life's experience you have the more this chapter will come in handy. Whether, or not you receive this, when you are truly in love, your guards are down, your walls are down, and your doors are wide open. This is not a bad thing if you want to risk being in love and loved. What makes it a bad thing is you don't exercise godly wisdom with your wall down and your doors open. We as sisters are communicators; we love to express ourselves. You can count the number on one hand how many sisters who don't talk much. That being said, it's not because she can't talk or doesn't want to talk, she just haven't found or ran into that person to whom she wants to talk. Believe me, she, too, has a lot to say, and probably more.

Let me first review this wonderfully new relationship where everything is new to the both of you, or should be. We will assume you never before knew one another, or if you did, you didn't know one another like you know one another now. You were, perhaps, just acquaintants, or friends of friends. He was not in your circle of friends or even ran in the crowds that you were associated. One day you woke up and it was like none other. You got that phone call or whatever, and now you are in a courtship and your head is in the clouds, or should be. Everything about him is interesting, and everything about you is interesting, from your hair, to your eyes, your hands and your pigeon-toe walk. Your laughter is new; your smile is too. Whatever you want he will get it for you. You talk about what you like and what you don't like. You talk about places you have been and places you want to go. You talk about people you have met and people you want to meet. You talk about restaurants and parks, schools, vacations, money and jobs, movies and favorites stores. You talk about clothes, styles, cars, houses, animals, children, parents, his family, your family, distant relatives, friends, church, God, dreams and aspirations, etc. You should be talking now more and more.

I told you, you need a new phone plan, because if you are courting as Christian court, all you are suppose to be doing is talking to help become more acquainted with this person, and about your future together as husband and wife. If you are not talking, that could really be a bad thing. You don't want to end up saying you wish you had talked about this or talked about that. I have included a list in this book; however, I hope that list has encouraged you to create your own list. Yes, you will or should be doing a lot of things together to help the process, but you know by now that sex is not one of them.

Everything about him should turn you on, from his cool walk, to his smooth voice, his laughter, his eyes, his interests, skills, etc. You have talked and talked and now you may be six months to a year before you walk down that aisle and you are really getting ready to do some serious talking, without thinking. When you talk and don't think before you talk you are not using what is called wisdom. Did you just meet this man or what? There are things you wouldn't tell a stranger but you will tell him, and you just met him. Think about it! Ok, so you said I'll marry you, but wait a minute, you haven't made it to the altar yet. I am on your side and I don't just want to help get you to the altar, but hope to say some things that will help you have a wonderful and successful Christian marriage if this is what you want as well. I'm sure by now, someone may have already told you don't talk too much and don't tell all of your business. If this is true, then here is your second, third or fourth confirmation.

God loves you and he wants you to know what he thinks about talking too much. Let me use this to help paint a picture of the consequences of doing so. When most kids were growing up and did bad things that parents felt required chastising, the parent would say go out in the yard and bring me a switch because you're going to get a whipping. Oh no, not again, you were thinking. So as a child who was thinking about the after the fact painful consequences, would go outside and find the smallest, littlest switch they could find and bring it back to momma, or grandma, or who ever sent them out to get the switch. What am I saying, the child never brought back a big stick that would bring them everlasting pain for days and weeks to come. They would bring back the smallest switch they could find, so that they could be assured that the switch wouldn't bring much pain.

What I am trying to say is some things that you may talk about in your courtship won't surely bring you much pain or regret, but there are some conversation that you may innocently share in the newness of your courtship that will be like going outside and bringing in the biggest stick you could find. And, if you are not careful, it will be the stick that will break you if you don't have much grace. The hardest part of getting the whipping is the pain came from the switch you chose. Nothing hurts more than the words "I told you so." In fact, it may be the weapon he uses later to pierce your soul and break your heart.

Nevertheless, if you have already made this mistake, remember, forgiveness is the sweetest revenge. Take heart and be strong. God still has your back when the devil reminds you of your past; just remind him of his future.

In the meantime remember God gave us two ears but only one mouth. Some people say that's because He wanted us to spend twice as much time listening than talking. Others claim it's because He knew that listening was twice as hard. Let your words be few, don't forget silence is golden.

Some Tips:
- Try not to use the words I've never received a dozen of red roses before, or I never had a candlelight dinner. For those of you who were in previous relationships or marriage, these are intimate romantic things that are or should be common between a man and a woman in a courtship. If you skipped that part or your past relationship didn't have such experience, it may be construed that you were maybe somehow not worthy of such treatment. So if you have not experience this before, just say things like, "Thank you for giving me my favorite flowers, and the candlelight dinner was wonderful. I would really like for us to do this more often. I love the way you read my mind." Now, you are giving him praise, for being taken to a place that has brought you pleasure and delight. He will look for other candlelight places to take you. It will become part of

what you do in your new relationship. You are expressing to him how you want to be treated, not reminded him of how you have not been treated. It is also guiding the relationship into a positive role setting direction. It's not a bad thing, and don't abuse the information.

• Subjects that I suggest not be talked on too early on in your relationship are life insurance amounts, monetary settlements, insurance payoff from a previous deceased spouse or child, pensions or social security payments. Marrying a man is not a retirement plan. If he has it like that, that's one lest gray hair and you're very fortunate. However, keep some things private 'til after the marriage. Keep in mind some money issues will need to be discussed, so that you know how the family will be supported financially. You decide what's important before you speak all your mind.

• Don't be foolish and kick true friends to the curb such as your talking buddy who listens to everything, from a new website you found, to sharing grocery coupons, family issues, personal issues, church and job stuff. So you got a new love and you talk to him every waking hour. Here's another tip, hold on to all your good old friends, and make a few new friends along the way.

• Marrying a man is not marrying a free consultation plan. Don't dump that garbage [*your old issues*] on him, especially if you have been married before or have baby daddy drama, even if it's his profession. You are courting, not in court. Remember, everything new gets old including a new relationship.

• Notice I did not talk much on sex. This, too, is a no-no. You don't have to listen or read this section but you will be glad you did. You know some sisters act like they never did a thing. If he believes you to be so, you may choose to let your mate know that you are not a virgin. Honesty is vitally important when you began a new marriage. Another no-no is to go into the details of past relationship after you lost your virginity. Remember: You are a Christian now, 2 Corinthians 5:17 Therefore, if any man be in Christ, he is a new creature: old things are passed away; behold, all things are become new – including your new relationship. Don't taint it with old past relationships.

• It is not cute, sexy, or wise to say, "I've had at least thirty-five boyfriends." If you had sex once, you are experienced. You don't have to say how experienced which make him feel like he's marrying a whorish woman. Later, he will wonder could he satisfy you sexually. Also, should you go into how many relationship you have had, the conversation will surely lead into sexual detailed accounts of these relationships, which may range from as early as your teen years through adulthood. You may be quite experienced and have a lot to say. This topic will lead to talking about fetishes and hot spots and body parts, and what turn you on, and what turn you off sexually. It will lead to bedroom conversation. If you have never been in his, and he has never been in yours, it is a good thing.

• It will mess with his head, and you may live to regret ever telling him your past. This subject will open the door of temptation to test you to see if you are a sample or a saint. This is not a topic you should have with your soon to be husband. He is one man, coming behind many men [*or your former or deceased husband*] who had sex with you. If you were raped and have not had counseling, you need to do so before you become sexually active with your husband. The sexual act itself may cause flash back that will harm your sexual relationship with your new husband. You may not be aware of how being sexually assaulted affected your mind [*being previous sexually active, voluntarily or involuntarily through some violent sexual act*] until you get into a committed relationship with just one person in marriage. When you talk on your past sexual experiences bad or good, you leave the door open for mean-spirited remarks hurled towards your past when things may not go so well in the bed or in the marriage. You may be blamed for the lack of sexual satisfaction, because they may try and convince you that one man is not enough for you, thereby becoming a victim twice.

• Save some conversations for marriage. Don't overwhelm him with your past, focus instead on your future. While getting to know him, allow time to bond.

• Something said prematurely can and will form into an arrow when returned to you because you gave him ammunition. Nothing hurts more than giving the individual the weapon of choice. Bringing your past into your new and exciting future will be harmful to you, and your new relationship.

- It could be the other way around, but you innocently, put your foot in your mouth when you talked too much during your courtship, trying to be open and honest. Speaking everything on your mind is foolish, not wise. This was your past, and should not be part of your future. If you are not a virgin, and only had one sexual relationship bad or good, you should never discuss it. This is a no-no rule. There is no rule that says, you must tell everything to begin a new relationship.
- Give your husband his props in your new committed sexual relationship when you are married, and let there not be anything for him to compare.
- Past sexual relationships good or bad should never be discussed, whether or not you were previously married or not.
- Being open and honest should be the rule of thumb in a new relationship, but being open about your past, should not be an option to secure your future. Bury the past, and embrace the presence and let God take care of your future. Silence is golden. Let your words be few.

RULE 13:

You Can be a Cinderella

[*Modern Day Spiritual Cinderella - Told my way*]

"By humility and the fear of Yahuah [יהוה] are riches, and honour, and life" Proverb 22:4

Practically, every little American girl has been introduced to the fairy-tale story about Cinderella. The word Cinderella has come to mean one whose attributes are unrecognized, or one who unexpectedly achieves recognitions or success after a period of obscurity and neglect. However, for the possibilities of someone not knowing this story, Cinderella is a popular fairy tale embodying a classic folk tale of unjust oppression, and triumphant reward. Cinderella is a young woman living in unfortunate circumstances which suddenly changed to remarkable fortune. Even in the worst of circumstances – the death of her mother, her father remarrying a wicked woman with two daughters of equal fame – she was still able to keep her unparalleled goodness and sweet temper.

The Prince invited all the ladies of the land to a ball so he could choose a wife...note he was looking for a wife. The stepsisters were preparing to go to the ball and Cinderella had to assist them in their preparation. They taunted her by saying a maid could never attend a ball.

Cinderella really desired to go, so her fairy godmother assisted her by turning a pumpkin into a coach, mice into horses, a rat into a coachman, a lizard into footmen. The fairy godmother changed Cinderella rags into a beautiful ball gown, with glass slippers to give that finishing touch. The

Prince falls in love with her, marries her and they live forever in his palace. Now let's visit a modern day [*spiritual*] Cinderella and her season of love. For by humility and the fear of the Lord are riches, and honor, and life.

Your season will begin with miraculous events ushering you to a new promotion. Whatever you already have will begin to take on life. God begins by using what you already have to bless you. Your surrounding will began to change. Blessings will come from everywhere. You won't need a fairy godmother, a sugar daddy, or hit the lottery. You will not need to dot all your i's or cross all your t's. What you have done in secret, God is about to reward you in the open. Blessings are going to run ahead of you, and wait for you to get there. The ball is a set up for your enemies, who are going to be summoned by God almighty and given a V.I.P. invitation to witness your season of love. They must be present to fulfill the scripture; "Thou preparest a table before me in the presence of mine enemies; their presence is demanded to see the goodness of the Lord. They will see, and not be able to taste or enjoy the goodness of the Lord" [Psalm 23:5].

Just as Cinderella had to obey the rules and return back home before midnight, you must enjoy your season as it will not last forever. Seasons come and go. Do not forget earthly gifts are temporal, never forget where you come from, and obey and listen to those who love you and care about your well-being and future. The Modern Day Spiritual Cinderella knows that in the multitude of counselors there is safety. She will listen to her Pastor, the church mothers, and those who God placed in her life. Because of her obedience, she will not be made ashamed.

Cinderella was unrecognized by her stepsisters at the ball. People think they know you, but they really don't know who you are. That part is irrelevant as long as you know who and whose you are. Cinderella knew who she was in rags and in beautiful clothes. People will miss the [*ball*] preview of your season. They will be looking at you all the time but will not see you as you change right before their eyes from worldly rags to spiritual riches. By the time they recognize the spiritual metamorphosis of your life you will be in your next season.

Never forget the words of the Blesser, Jesus Christ. Do not forget the words of your Heavenly Father: "He is the giver of every good and perfect gift." When we obey his words, we will not be made ashamed or make him ashamed. Do not get so caught up with the blessing that you disobey the

Blesser. Cinderella made it to the ball; the entire court was entranced by her, especially the prince who never left her side. Cinderella almost forgot a cloud rule; her head was so in the clouds with the prince that her foot almost slipped. She lost track of time and left only at the final stroke of midnight, and one of her glass slippers was left behind on the palace steps in her haste to obey. Can you imagine how her foot almost slipped? Maybe your foot almost slipped, but goodness and mercy will have your back. It was all good. She left behind a testimony of obedience. Obedience kept her from being made a fool. The word of her godmother kept her from being made ashamed. If you obey the words of wisdom, you too will not be made ashamed.

The prince chased her outside the palace. When the prince asked the guards had they seen her, they replied we saw a single country maid leave. The prince pocketed the slipper and vowed to find and marry the girl to whom it belonged. God will hide you in your unperfected state. She left with her good name intact even though she had to run. Run my sister, run, and don't be afraid to run if you have to. Cinderella ran from the prince. She left at the right time, and she left leaving something on his mind. How many of you would have had the strength to run from a prince? Well, don't worry. God won't put more on you than you are able to bear. 1 Corinthians 10:13 encourages us that "There hath no temptation taken you but such as is common to man: but God is faithful, who will not suffer you to be tempted above that ye are able; but will with the temptation also make a way to escape, that ye may be able to bear it." Keep your good name; and your testimony. Get in a hurry because your blessing is on the way. What God has for you will be yours in due season.

Don't let your good be evil spoken of [Romans 14:16]. Cinderella kept the other slipper which had not disappeared when the spell had broken. Favor ain't fair. When things are suppose to go against you, they will end up in your favor. The spell was supposed to turn everything back to the original state, but her glass slippers remained glass slippers. Your testimony will keep by the power of the Holy Ghost. You too, can be twice a virgin. You don't have to prove to anyone whether or not you are a virgin and whether you have ever known a man; or twice a virgin and have been sexually active in the past. The Holy Spirit has keeping power and when you've got the real thing and he's got the real thing it will remain when you are together and when you are a part.

Take note: the prince came to Cinderella. He was the pursuer, and when he found her she was at home looking like she looked no doubt every day. Just a plain Jane, but the prince saw beyond the beautiful ball gown and the glass slipper, he saw and found a wife, the desire of his heart. He knew he could safely trust in her.

She was a rare gem, something that wasn't easy to find, and worth looking for. The prince searched the entire villa, stopping here and there, looking everywhere trying the slipper on all the young women in the land. Yes, the prince was slow in coming. But he that shall come, will come and will not tarry. Your prince may be talking to this sister, and that sister, but don't sweat it, he's just looking for the right one. Trust the God that's in him. He won't be satisfied until he arrives at your door.

When the prince arrived at Cinderella's home, the stepsisters [*haterators*] tried in vain to fit the glass slippers. Cinderella asked to try on the glass slippers as well. The stepsisters taunted her for even having the audacity to want to try on the slipper. It was a set-up right before their eyes the slipper fit perfectly. Then Cinderella produced the other slipper for good measure. The stepsister's begged forgiveness and Cinderella forgave them for their cruelties. When a man's ways please the Lord, he makes even his enemies to be at peace with him.

Take notice: Cinderella had a witness, the matching slipper. You have a witness inside you, the Holy Spirit. The same spirit he has should be the same spirit you have. The Holy Spirit will be a witness that you two have that self same spirit. God commands that you be equally yoked with a believer. The Holy Spirit will give you a testimony that he is able to keep you from falling, because no weapon formed against you shall prosper, no spell, no haterators, no issues will stop your blessing and your pulchritudinous prince from looking for you.

When a man is looking for a wife, he's looking for the perfect fit. Someone he can take home and give all his worldly goods. You don't have to worry whether the shoe will fit; he'll know and the Holy Ghost in you will be a witness that you have the goods. The shoe will be a perfect fit. If God sent the right man to you to be his wife, he already knows you both will be satisfied. It's a God thing. He doesn't make mistakes; we do.

Cinderella returned to the palace where she married the Prince. You may have a past of pumpkins, and lizards, and mice and a multitude of issues that the devil want to use against you to say see, nothing good is possible for you. All things are possible, if you only believe. God can take all your pumpkins, lizards, mice, issues and etc., and make miracles out of your mistakes. Remember the cloud rules. Clouds come to pass but don't last. If we were to look at Cinderella's characteristics we could very closely see the attributes of the virtuous woman.

So, some of you may still have your reservations about this Cinderella story, and say no one can be all that. Well, I beg your pardon! There are thousands of modern day virtuous spiritual Cinderellas [*called spiritual Ruths*] who excels them all.

Look at the many attributes of Cinderella
- She never looked down on anyone or anything.
- She had inner and outer beauty
- She was loved by the least and unlikely sorts
- She was not a lazy person
- She wasn't selfish; she shared what she had, of herself and her substance
- She had a wonderful *attitude* which took her to a higher *altitude* in life
- She didn't blame others for her temporarily misfortune
- She used what she had, until she could do better, and she did
- She was a forgiving person, never holding a grudge
- She allowed herself to love and be loved
- She preferred her sister over herself
- She was picked on to be picked out
- She waited until her changed came
- She was obedient to her superiors
- She had an inner hope, that some sweet day she would be in a better place.
- She did her best all the time, and was called upon even the more
- She was never idle nor in others folks business; she was too busy serving others
- She was loving and caring always taking care of others
- She was always herself; she didn't try to be anyone else
- She had much humility in spite of her adversity

- She may have lived in the ghetto, hole in the wall, but the ghetto wasn't in her
- She was envied even when she didn't have stuff and things
- She was laughed at and talked about but she surpassed them all
- She didn't have a loving mother, but she loved the mother she had
- She didn't have a loving family, but she loved the family she had
- She didn't stop being who she was after she got married
- She was elevated and promoted to a higher level
- She was a Shero in the books, and her name is still ringing of her fame
- Her reputation precedes her, and she is still desired of kings everywhere
- She can't be substituted; only she can fill such honorable shoes
- She's not heady or high-minded, but humble and kindhearted
- She has a good name
- She's a good thing, a precious jewel; her king is searching for her even now
- She waited patiently, in her own house, until he arrived at her door
- She didn't look for the king; the king came looking for her and found her
- She didn't have to be seen or heard, she was just in the right place at the right time. It was her season. She was already blessed and highly favored.
- She forgave those who hurt her the most; forgiveness comes before promotion. The last thing Jesus did on the cross before he gave up the ghost was to forgive those who didn't know who He was, before he was promoted.
- Someone said, When you don't forgive it's like drinking poison and expecting the other person that you can't forgive to die.

And, yes, they are all that, because they are one in a million. Have you noticed, they all have a Cinderella testimony? Yes! You can have one, too, because all things are possible if you only believe. If you think you can, you can; and if you think you can't you're probably right, too.

RULE 14:

Give God A Raise With Your Praise In Prayer

"Let the high praises of God be in [*your*] mouth" Psalm 149:6

Jesus said, "But seek ye first the kingdom of God, and his righteousness; and all these things shall be added unto you" Matthew 6:33. Prayer is the communication between the creature and the creator. It is the vehicle you need to stay in touch with your God. When you truly love someone you talk all the time, talk, talk, talk, morning noon, and night. What kind of relationship do you think you would have with your new husband, if after marriage your excessive talking time dwindled from six hours a day to about six minutes a day? You use to talk for breakfast, lunch, and dinner, and now you just say good morning and good night. You figure, how long would your relationship last. How about God? Before your prince came, you were always in God's face. You were in Sunday school, Sunday worship service, prayer service, Bible study, conventions and councils. Your conversations—your Christian lifestyle—were about God. He did this, and God did that, and how wonderful God is. Did God change or did you change?

Don't forget…he's the one that said, "No good thing would I withhold from them that love him." Are you going to kick him to the curb or are you going to give God a raise in your praise and in your prayer life. This is one rule, you can't afford to omit. Stay committed to your prayer life, so you can stay connected to your eternal source. It was God that blessed you to be one in a million. God wants to be all up in your business. He wants to be part of your life in every intimate way. He wants to talk to you, so he can order your footsteps along the way.

The following suggestions are designed to encourage you to develop and spend quality time with God. Start by bringing some things along to discuss with him: Don't forget your Bible, a song, and your prayer list. Find a place where the two of you won't be disturbed.

Preparation – Beginning Prayer: Ask God to help you spend this time profitably with him. Ask his guidance. Give yourself to him a predetermined amount of time.

Confession – Spend a couple of minutes going over with him recent sins which weigh on you. Don't dredge up old ones. He is far more willing to forgive then you are to ask. 1 John 1:9

Praise, thanksgiving and adoration – Sing to the Lord using a hymnal or some choruses you know. Lift up your voice in praise. It's just the two of you. Now thank him for his goodness, kindness and tender mercies. There is a special sense in which God "inhabits" [KJV] [Psalm 22:3]. As your heart begins to adore him, you'll sense his presence more deeply.

There is a song that goes like this: "I know what prayer can do. Prayer has brought me through." Right now I'm concerned about you; you ought to pray some, too. Pray in the morning, anytime of the day. Prayer will keep that devil, keep that devil away. I know, I know, I know what prayer can do.

You are God's good thing! Courtship can be considered your probationary season. You are not the mother of Jesus. This engagement does not mean you are his wife. When you pass the test, you will have a testimony which you rarely hear these days, but you are going to change that with the help of God and this book. When you bless God in your daily walk you give God a raise in your praise and in your prayer life.

RULE 15:

Special Notes For Second Time Married Or Non-Virgins

Maybe it's no secret you are not a virgin. You've been around a few years. high school days have evolved into years. Maybe as many as ten, twenty or thirty years. Okay, so who's counting? You have grown children, and even perhaps grandchildren and you feel awkward just holding hands. You have been there and done that, it's no secret. You will ask yourself, how can I be sure we will be compatible, you know, in the bedroom? I've been holding out, waiting for my change and my chance, and now it's here. I use to date Tom, Dick and Harry and I didn't have to wonder, or maybe you were married for many years and was used to only one partner. You had sex that was part of the relationship. Now you are concerned with a natural life's reality question. You say, I've given my life to Christ and I have chosen to wait on God. Now What? How can I be sure that I will be happy or satisfied in that area?

That's a great question and you can't be sure. But, you can be sure of this one thing. If you are confident that God has designed him to be your soul mate, God's choice and not your choosing, you will be sure on that night, and nights to come he will be better than you expect, because God Did It! You will say, like the song: Oh, Lord, I just want to thank you. I want to thank you, for being so good to me.

But until that time, be extra careful against temptation. Keep decent hours of courtship. Don't trust your emotions; it's untrustworthy when your head is in the clouds. God want to be intimate and real in our daily lives. He is a loving and a passionate creator. Yes, and he is even concern about our passions, he knows our down sitting and our uprising. Don't trust yourself. Our flesh cannot be trusted. Don't put confidence in the flesh. So what you're grown. We are not talking about age. We're talking about love. For you who failed the test of this rule, and have gotten yourself into a mess, well, it's just right for God. You are still worth the wait. The only way he will know if you are worth the wait and that is he just has to wait and see. If he is as crazy about you as he say, then make him prove it. He will love you even more for it. He will respect you even more and hold you up in high esteem, convinced that he has made the right choice making you his wife. King Solomon had seven hundred wives, princesses, and three hundred concubines, yet this Shulamite maiden held her testimony; he said, "There is no spoil in thee."

Another good Cloud Rule is simply not to get too comfortable. Don't be the next humpty dumpty that had a great fall. Don't be so easy, or should I say silly as described in 2 Timothy 3 "...for of this sort are they which creep into houses, and lead captive silly women laden with sins, led away with divers lusts."

Silly means: *simple, foolish, weak-headed, weak-minded, witless, empty-headed, unwise, irrational and etc*. Don't set yourself up to be raped. Many of your sisters have trusted their fiancé to the depth of taking showers in their homes, allowing their feet to be washed and massaged, making their beds, sleeping overnight, or whatever the case may be as if they were already married. Assert yourself and insist on being treated with respect. Not by what you say, but by what you do. You set the respect pace. This rule will be extremely valuable when you are married.

Don't be afraid to refuse an invitation to sleep over just because you may live an hour or so away. If he brought you to his house, insist on him taking you home. Leave an extra hour early so you can have a tomorrow. The smart thing to do is not allow yourself to be kept out so late that when he takes you back home, he may want to sleep over at your place. Just talk him back home on the phone. If you do it once, what reason will you have to not let it happen again? A very important note here is, even when you innocently do things, it's still not appropriate. Don't let your good be evil spoken of. 1 Thessalonians 5:22 reminds us to "Abstain from all appearance of evil." Don't give your man any reason to doubt your good name. Never let him sleep over for your name sake and Christ sake. If he loves you, he will go home, period.

You haven't made it to the altar yet! And don't take for granted for one moment that it's a done deal. This is one of the reasons this book was written, many of our sister's thought it was a done deal and gave it up [*had sexual intercourse*] and it was disastrous to say the least. Even though they married, the relationship grew even worse.

You have got the goods; in fact, the more he presses you, emphatically confirms what you have is worth the wait. It's a good thing, precious, priceless and it belongs to you. This applies to you even if you are not a virgin. Just being a Christian makes you pure again in the eyes of God when you commit your body and life to Christ to abstain from fornication and the very appearance of evil by living a life of abstinence. In fact, being twice a virgin carries a heavier weight of responsibility because you know what you are waiting for. You have been there and done that, and you know what to do and how to do it.

The pressure on you to succumb to the very act of sexual iniquity outside of marriage carries a heavier responsibility for those that know about sex from experience. It's like knowing what strawberry ice-cream taste like. Once you know, you know. The devil wants to make you fall, so he can accuse the Holy Spirit of not having enough power to keep you. The devil is a liar. My sister, let me assure you the Holy Spirit has more than enough power to keep you from falling if you want to be kept.

You're twice a virgin now, and it's by your conscious decision, and the keeping power of the Spirit of God. Simply because you chose to respect your body, the temple of the Holy Spirit, it is then that you understand the honor the Father has bestowed upon you to become a Christian bride to be.

1 John 1:9 promises forgiveness if you confess your past sins. Consult with your pastor; he is the shepherd of your soul. If your pastor is your parent, many times it's proper to be counseled by another pastor. As a pastor's daughter, it was a family rule, that we could take our issues to another pastor for help. In my opinion, the pastor's family, need a pastor. It is not a rule, but sometime helpful. So you have messed up, and a mess is a mess, no matter how big or small it is. Get up from there, repent, confess and sin no more. Now you are still worth the wait. Get back in God's grace. Stay away from what got you there in the first place. If you are still in the relationship and are going to get married, you are not to continue in sin. The

Apostle Paul asked, "Shall I continue in sin that grace may abound?" The answer was an emphatic No! If you can't wait, go to the courthouse make it legal. Have a reception later. Get right with God and he will bless you. Proverb 22:1 says, "A good name is rather to be chosen than great riches, and loving favour rather than silver and good." Only the test of time will tell if you are worth the wait, and that is you will make him wait.

Chicago's former Mayor Harold Washington's famous quote was, "I have places to go, things to do and people to see." My sister, you too have places to go, things to do and people to see. You don't have time to fool around, twiddle your thumbs, or act like the Mrs. which you are not. NO, you are not the Mrs., so don't be cajoled into doing chores of a housewife because he prematurely call you "wife." Don't let him take you to his house to wash his last week dishes, vacuum his floors, wash his laundry.

You are not his wife. This is your special time to be wooed. The only chore he should have in his mind is to sweep you off your feet. It's your time to wear the ring on your finger, not wash the ring off his tub. You have the rest of your life to wash his dirty ring around the collar, or ring around the tub. If you get it right, you'll have the man and the ring and everything in between. In fact, stay out of his bedroom, bathroom, and kitchen.

Let me give you a very personal testimony during my courtship. There was a period of time during my courtship that I found myself being lead of the Holy Ghost to begin fasting. I never stopped my prayer life; in fact, I had more to pray about, but, fasting, come on. I was courting. Everyday my fiancé was taking me to either breakfast or dinner, depending on our schedules. I was eating in places I had only dreamed.

The best pancake houses and candlelight eating; I was on Cloud Nine. Why in heavens sake, do I need to do all this fasting? First the fasting was just casual, and then I was compelled to continue on a regular basis with no apparent reasoning. I dared not question the Holy Spirit, but my flesh was really getting a little impatient with all this fasting. I felt this was the proper time to eat, drink and be merry. On top of that, I asked my fiancé [*the preacher*] to fast with me. He said to me there was no reason for him to fast since I was the one getting promoted. He was messing with my mind. I know exactly what you are thinking, the nerve of him to say such a thing to me. Personally, I was extremely insulted at the time. Needless to say, we did quickly get over it with a few laughs. He was right, I was getting promoted. I didn't choose him, he chose me. Remember King Solomon. Out of all the wives and concubines he had, why the Shulamite maiden. She was about to get promoted.

The fasting was an act of obedience to remain good. It had nothing to do with the Elder; I was the good thing that was going to be his helpmate because God was going to enlarge his territory as he transitioned into the pastorate. At the time of our courtship, he was not a pastor.

So my sister, if the Holy Spirit calls you on a fast, obey his voice. It wasn't about me falling; it was about me rising to another level. Don't have your head so in the clouds that you cannot hear the voice of the Holy Spirit. In fact, this is a time, when you should be more sensitive to the voice of your Savior. The foreknowledge of the Holy Spirit already knew I wasn't going to fall, because I'm here today. The Holy Spirit already knew that I loved him enough that whatever he asked me to do I would obey. You have to already have it like that with your love for Jesus Christ. Someone said, your test and trials are not for you, but for others. I take great joy in knowing that if this testimony blesses you, then surely my fasting was not in vain. Praise our God! Nothing and no one should come between you and your savior, not even the love of your life. This life is temporal but life with Jesus is eternal.

When you love God and keep his commandments, you're about to get promoted. I, too, like the Shulamite maiden had a lot of issues. There were so many other women out there fairer than I. They were saved and sanctified virgins with no children, the edumacated, [*educated*] sisters, sisters with the six-figure bank account, fine cars and clothes to boot, and sisters who still had their coke cola bottle figure. And here I was in a place in my life where I had been reduced to a divorced welfare mom, with nine minor children to raise alone. I lost my $200,000 home in South Holland, Illinois, and a host of other issues. All the while, I never lost my praise. I continue to obey the Holy Spirit and fast. I can't remember when I was able to resume my ordinary eating habits, but I can tell you there was a spiritual warfare going on out of this world. Later, the Holy Ghost gave me the reason for all that fasting, and I'm so humble to say, it wasn't for me per say, but for you who are reading this book. God brought back to my remembrance the scripture about the man that finds a wife finds a good thing. [*good – whole, unblemished, blameless, exemplary, guiltless, pure, virtuous, irreprehensible, sound, righteous, lily-white, conforming to a high standard of morality or virtue, behaving in an acceptable or desirable manner*].

I feel the preacher talking now. If God declares something good, it is his responsibility to preserve and keep that which he declared to be good. Let me repeat that. It is God's responsibility to preserve and keep us from falling. Daughter of excellence, I hope after you read, digest, and finish eating the gospel of this book, your soul mate will be good enough for you. God said to me the fast was the conditioning process, on which his promise word was to be performed. If something doesn't remain good, [*it will spoil*] becoming bad or evil and is unprofitable and has lost its value [*salt*] and reputation as being good. Don't be like the fool in Psalm 14 who said in his heart there is no God.

King Solomon is a type of Christ, and the Shulamite maiden represents the church. The church is the bride of Jesus Christ that he went away to prepare a place for. Jesus blood has redeemed a great many daughters and he's still pursuing more daughters of excellence to show forth his praises, to a wicked and perverse generation. There are many Christian sisters that excel them all, and my sister there is still room for one more. One day he will return for his bride the church who will present herself without spot or wrinkle or any such thing. Your new husband will say like King Solomon Thou art all fair, my love there is NO SPOT [*spoil*] in thee [Solomon 4:7]. His heart doth safely trust in her and he will have no need of spoil. You are worth the wait, because the God in you doesn't pacify, He satisfies.

RULE 16:

Pass The Salt, Please

"Ye are the salt of the earth:
but if the salt have lost his savour, wherewith shall it be salted?
It is thenceforth good for nothing." Matthew 5:13

One day I was not minding my own business and found myself stooping down to my mother's bedroom door trying to hear a conversation that I was not invited too. Just for the record, I was about nine or ten years old. My mom was in her bedroom talking to my big sisters about something. I assumed it was super important because she was speaking so quietly. I just had to put my ear close to the door to hear, and then before I knew it, the door flew open and I was in trouble with a capital "T."

I was caught guilty, red handed, hands down, get the belt and start praying. I can just imagine the expression on my face, horrified at being caught eavesdropping at momma's door. However, all I can remember was my mom saying to me that she was having a big girl's talk and when I get bigger one day, she was going to have the same talk with me. She said it with such love and kindness that I was immediately at peace with her words and convinced that she would keep her promise. I never again tried to overhear or eavesdrop any conversations that she had with my big sisters because I was waiting for that big day when she was going to sit me down and talk to me about big girl stuff.

This chapter is most important to me because I will never know all the hands this book will touch, the minds this book will influence, or all the hearts it will change for Christ sake. Therefore, to you my sister who may not have had the mother, sister or girlfriend to sit you down and talk to you about big girl stuff, I hope this book has enlightened, encouraged and equipped you for the beautiful journey ahead.

You already know that a man that finds a wife finds a good thing. Christian sisters need to be reminded that we are the salt of the earth, and if we are not fulfilling our purpose, we are good for nothing. Gods' children are called to be Salt. Salt is a preservative. The salt in every Christian sister is the word of God. It will keep you, if you want to be kept. If a Christian sister doesn't keep herself 'til marriage she has no salt and is good for nothing, except, you know, a free sample. Remember you were picked out to be shined upon. I am convinced that there are many dignified sisters [including our virtuous sisters who have chosen to be pure again. Those who will keep their dresses down and their undergarments up—those sisters that still wear them—for that precious and special day!

All she needed was [*some spiritual seasoning salt*] a big sister talk, someone to help her alone the way.

I have often told my daughters, I'm not trying to win a popularity contest in being your friend. My first responsibility is to be your parent; we can be friends later. To you my sister, this book will probably not win a popularity contest, but I hope at least you know you have a new friend, i.e., someone who will tell you the truth. You can do with it as you please. A true friend will feel ashamed seeing their friend doing something out of character. They would at least say something or find a way to express their opinions, and have a reasonable conversation as to why their friend could have or should have done things differently. Well, this book is that friend, I have felt so much shame when I look at my sisters especially in the Christian community and see how she has devalued herself in so many ways. I just wanted to say something, so I wrote the book to see if I could just help a sister out!

Mark 9:50 says, "Salt is good: but if the salt has lost his saltiness, wherewith will ye season it? Have salt in yourselves." You've got to give God something to work with. Get the word in you by reading your Bible, and speak the word to yourself when you need it.

If the word's not there, hidden in your heart, you'll be like the bird who gave the cat his last feather for a worm. Don't trade a feather [*your good thing*] for a worm.

This saying comes from a story about a bird and a cat. A conniving cat made a deal with a trifling, lazy bird who didn't want to get up early to get his own worms for his daily survival. The cat [*a bird's natural enemy*] made a deal with the bird by convincing him to give up one feather for every worm he would give him. Sounds good to me thought the bird, I have plenty of feathers and some to spare. So they had a cozy relationship, he had temporary peace with his natural enemy. As long as he would provide a feather, the cat would give him a worm. The bird got to eat without working, and the cat seemingly did all the work for nothing, providing food for the bird every time the bird wanted to eat. I mean after all, one would think, what can a cat do with something he don't need or can use like feathers? Yet it was exactly what the cat wanted because he had a devious scheme.

So after Mr. Cat had been hustling worms a long time, all that hard work paid off. [*I mean even the Bible says, if a man doesn't work he shouldn't eat. Ok, I just had to put that in there.*] Mr. Cat had patience and longsuffering. Why did the cat allow the bird to live free from all his cares of toiling for worms, not even having to watch his back?

Tweet, tweet sings the now fat juicy birdie, awaiting for another worm from Mr. Cat. Mr. Cat says to the bird, you know the deal, no feather, no worm. So the bird gives his last feather to the cat, and the rest is history. The cat ate the fat delicious [*silly*] bird for supper. Common sense would assume that the bird did run, but could not get away. He foolishly sold himself to the cat, by giving up the first feather. It was just a matter of time that the bird would be consumed by the cat. God created the bird with feathers to fly away when danger was near. But because the bird was lazy, and unappreciative of his most valuable assets, he gave it away for something he could have gotten for himself.

This common saying, trading a feather for a worm, has a serious reference to giving up something precious and valuable for temporal thrills and gratifications, like hamburgers and watches, presents, stuff and things, and a little conversation. If you're not careful, and he's a Mr. Cat in disguise, one day you will have no power to resist the devil. It will be payday, and you will pay up. As long as the bird had feathers he had power to escape the deadly paws of the cat and fly away. Greater is He that is within you, than he that is in the world. Christian sisters have power to escape from the clutches of the enemy. That cat was just like the devil. What does he want with your stuff? He doesn't need things like your good name, or your anointing, or your gifts or good looks and talents. You know what the devil wants? He wants the God in you. That's the good thing! Your good God. We pray that you, our sisters, don't trade your God for stuff and things.

1 Corinthians 10:13 encourages us that, "There hath no temptation taken you but such as is common to man: but God is faithful, who will not suffer you to be tempted above that ye are able; but will with the temptation also make a way to escape, that ye may be able to bear it." Don't trade your good name, by finding yourself in circles of those who are known to not have a good name, just because you want to have friends or be seen with certain people. If you want friends, go befriend those who are going in the same direction, and have the same mind you have. Don't trade your godliness for worldliness; it has a price. Every time you give it what it asks, you will pay something for it in return. That something will be paid with your soul. Remember the devil doesn't want your stuff and things, he has stuff and things that you know not of. He is the god of this world and can summons any designer demon to bring you stuff and things, but what he really desires most is the God in you. That's what you'll be trading, the God things.

You've heard the plea, "Baby, you don't have to do nothing, just say you'll be mine. I'll give you the world. I'll buy you diamond rings; just tell me what you want, I'll work two jobs, etc." Well, my sister all I will say is, if Mr. Cat is talking the talk, make him walk the walk. Tell him "That's good and fine and sign on the dotted line of the marriage license, cause until then, you are absolutely right, I don't have to do nothing, and I won't do a thing until then. So let's go pick out that diamond ring, set the date and get married."

You know by now, if you don't start your relationship out with godly and moral convictions you probably will be trading a many feathers for worthless worms and one day you won't be able to fly away. The cat [*Mr. smooth talker*] will lick his chops and have you for breakfast, lunch and dinner. It's important to remember that the godly mate that you have will be one that pleases God. God's plan is that together you will be heirs in the Kingdom of God. 1 Peter 3:7

"Likewise, ye husbands, dwell with them according to knowledge, giving honour unto the wife, as unto the weaker vessel, and as being heirs together of the grace of life." I pray that the salt which was passed on to me from my mother has in many ways been passed down to you within the pages of this book. With confidence I am assured that you too, now, have enough salt to share. "O LORD, I know that the way of man is not in himself: it is not in man that walketh to direct his steps" Jeremiah 10:23. "Blessed is the man that trusteth in the Lord, and whose hope the Lord is" Jeremiah 17:7. I pray this book is like salt to your soul and has been a blessing to you and those with whom you will share it. If you were a silly woman, I hope you are now sober and can read the handwriting on the wall. If you fall remember, it's always too soon to quit. It's never too late to get started again. If you wholeheartedly trust God and continue to put God first in your life, you will know without doubt that, "the blessing of Yahuah [יהוה], it maketh rich, and he addeth no sorrow with it" Proverb 10:22.

I pray my words have been seasoned with just enough salt, and will continue to be a lasting godly influence and blessing on your life. It is our desire and endeavor to bring glory to God while ultimately enlarging Christ's Kingdom with the gift of writing as God has blessed me.

YOU CAN DO IT! You have the power to lead him to the altar because, Greater is **he** that is within you than he that is in the world. Christian sisters you are the real jewels. The only kind you can't buy, and the only kind not for sale. You are rare and priceless, and when a Christian man finds you, God declared that he has found a good thing, and favor ain't for the cowards who won't commit.

There is nothing more attractive, appealing, encouraging, nothing more breathtaking, beautiful, magnificent, nothing more delightful, inspiring, elegant, nothing more lovely, stunning, and precious than a Christian sister boldly and graciously at the altar, blameless, and undefiled, standing before a Holy God and her godly man. He ain't seen nothing yet. You are truly the light of the world. You have showed up and Jesus is about to show out. Just give him a committed body and he will sanctify it.

> "Who Is Wise? He will realize these things, who is discerning?
> He will understand them.
> The ways of Yahuah [יהוה] are right; the righteous walk in them,
> but the rebellious stumble in them."
> Hosea 14:9

Now unto him that is able to keep you from falling, and to present you faultless before the presence of his glory with exceeding joy, To the only wise God our Saviour, be glory and majesty, dominion and power, both now and ever. Amen – *You are now officially a Cloud Rules Sister.*

My Personal Cloud Rule Commitment

Dear Jesus:

I. I _____ , a Christian Sister, commit myself to you, to be an ensample to the body of Jesus Christ.

II. I will always confess my sins.
   1 John 1:9

III. I will seek after wise council when I am in need.
   Proverb 1:5 – Proverb 24:6

IV. I will love you with my body, soul and spirit.
   John 14:23 – 1 Thessalonians 5:23

V. I will forgive those who hurt me.
   Matthew 6:14-15

VI. I will bless you every day.
   Psalm 34:1

VII. I will not let my good be evil spoken of.
   1 Corinthians 15:33

VIII. I will guard my ear, eye, and mouth gate.
   2 Peter 2:7

IX. I will trust your plans for my life and my future.
   Jeremiah 29:11

With the help and grace of God
I commit to myself, to be a Cloud Rules Sister, who will share
and pass these rules on to my sisters.

References

1. All Biblical references are from the King James Version of The Holy Bible [*public domain*], unless otherwise notated.

2. *New International Version Bible*, published by Zondervan, 1973, 1978, 1984

3. *Believer's Bible Commentary,* by William MacDonald, Edited by Arthur L. Farstad, Thomas Nelson Publishers, 1995

4. *Planning A Wedding To Remember,* by Beverly Clark, Publisher: Beverly Clark Collection, 2004

5. *Merriam-Webster's Collegiate Thesaurus*

6. U.S. Center For Disease Control and Prevention, 1600 Clifton Road, Atlanta, Georgia 30333.4018